I See Satan
Fall Like
Lightning

I See Satan
Fall Like
Lightning

René Girard

Translated, with a Foreword,
by James G. Williams

ORBIS BOOKS
Maryknoll, New York 10545

NOVALIS

GRACEWING

Eighth Printing, September 2009

Originally published as *Je vois Satan tomber comme l'éclair* by René Girard, copyright © 1999 by Éditions Grasset & Fasquelle, 61, rue des Saints-Pères, 75006 Paris, France.

English translation copyright © 2001 by Orbis Books.

Published in the United States by Orbis Books, Maryknoll, NY 10545-0308.

Published in Canada by Novalis, Saint Paul University, 223 Main Street, Ottawa, Ontario K1S 1C4.

Published in England by Gracewing, 2 Southern Avenue, Leominster, Herefordshire HR6 0QF.

All rights reserved.

No part of this publication may be reproduced or transmitted in any form or by any means, electronic or mechanical, including photocopying, recording or any information storage or retrieval system, without prior permission in writing from the publisher.

Queries regarding rights and permissions should be addressed to the publishers.

Manufactured in the United States of America.

Library of Congress Catalogue Card No.: 00-050182

Canadian Library Catalogue No.: C00-901789-5

ORBIS/ISBN 1-57075-319-9
NOVALIS/ISBN 2-89507-157-8
GRACEWING/ISBN 0 85244 290 4

I saw Satan fall like lightning from heaven . . .

—LUKE 10:18

Contents

Foreword

RENÉ GIRARD is the world's premier thinker about the role of violence in cultural origins, and about the Bible's illumination of these origins and our present human condition. Girard retired in 1996 after a distinguished teaching career, most recently at Stanford University. He is well known in his native France, where one of his books, *Things Hidden since the Foundation of the World,* provoked an intense debate among intellectuals and clergy in the late 1970s. The present work was repeatedly on the bestseller list in his native land after its publication in 1999. The attention his writings have drawn has been less dramatic in the English-speaking world than in France and the rest of Europe. However, his work is becoming more and more widely disseminated, influencing literary critics, theologians, psychologists, and many others who are concerned with what it means to be human in light of our biblical heritage.

René Girard offers a new way of seeing ourselves and our biblical heritage. His method is to begin, not with theology or the revelation of God, but with an understanding of human beings and human relations that the Bible and the early Christian tradition disclose. This understanding of humankind he articulates is an *anthropology* ("anthropologos," or discourse about what it means to be human).

Girard's anthropology focuses first on *desire* and its consequences. He calls it "mimetic desire" or "mimesis." It's a desire that comes into being through imitation of others. These others we imitate Girard calls "models," models of desire. He has also used the word "mediators," because they are "go-betweens," acting as agents between the individual imitating them and the world. There are various words in ordinary language that suggest what Girard is getting at:

for example, "heroes" and "role models." Even fashion models who "model" clothes are acting in this way for their public in the setting of clothing fashion. They present the clothing (bodies) that suggests what their admirers should desire.

The desire that lives through imitation almost always leads to conflict, and this conflict frequently leads to violence. The Bible unveils this process of imitative desire leading to conflict and violence, and its distinctive narratives reveal at the same time that God takes the part of victims. In the Gospels the process of unveiling or revelation is radicalized: God himself, the Word become flesh in Jesus, *becomes the victim.* The innocent victim who is crucified is vindicated through his resurrection from the dead. The disciples of Jesus finally undergo a complete conversion as they move from being lost in the mimetic desire of the crowd to imitating Christ, which occurs through their experience of Jesus' resurrection. Their conversion and the resurrection of Christ are two aspects of the same event.

To introduce the reader to what Girard offers in this, his most recent, book, I will present a series of questions and answers about his basic concepts. Getting a grasp of these concepts is essential for understanding what Girard has to say about desire, sacrifice, scapegoating, Satan, and other important topics. I hope this will be helpful, especially to the reader not already familiar with his thought.

1. *What is the chief identifying characteristic of human beings?*

Answer: To answer this at the anthropological level (leaving aside any question about the human soul or spirit): *mimetic desire.* The tenth commandment of the Decalogue in the books of Exodus and Deuteronomy addresses mimetic desire directly. The tenth commandment does not prohibit simply one desire, "coveting," but deals with desire as such. Desire is not an instinct; it is not something programmed into us, so it doesn't work like instincts in other creatures. It is rather a potential that must become activated for an infant to become human, and it becomes actual for the infant as he or she observes and imitates the other, the "neighbor." We want

what our neighbor possesses. We desire what our neighbor desires—
or what we think he or she desires. Of course, the chief neighbors,
or "near ones," for the infant are its parents. This desire that comes
into being through following models of desire is not bad; it is good.
To desire what models desire is necessary if the child is to be able
to learn and love and deal with the world. But it can and does lead
to conflict and violence.

2. How does mimetic desire lead to conflict and violence?

Answer: If our desire to be like a model is strong enough, if we
identify with that person closely enough, we will want to have what
the model has or be what the model is. If this is carried far enough
and if there are no safeguards braking desire (one of the functions of
religion and culture), then we become rivals of our models. Or we
compete with one another to become better imitators of the same
model, and we imitate our rivals even as we compete with them.
This rivalistic situation opens human societies to the possibility of
scandal.

3. What does Girard mean by "scandal"?

Answer: "Scandal" translates words from both Hebrew and Greek
that mean "stumbling block," something that people stumble over.
(It can also mean "trap" or "snare," a closely related meaning.)
Girard means specifically a situation that comes about when a person or a group of persons feel themselves blocked or obstructed as
they desire some specific object of power, prestige, or property that
their model possesses or is imagined to possess. They cannot obtain
it, either because they cannot displace the model and acquire what
he or she has or because the rivalry with others in the group is so intense that everyone prevents everyone else from succeeding. When
this kind of situation occurs often enough, there is an accumulation
of scandals to the point that those involved must "let off steam" or
the social fabric will burst. Then all those involved in this tangle of
rivalry turn their frustrated desire against a victim, someone who is
blamed, who is identified as an offender causing scandal.

The whole process of scandal developing to a breaking point is an unconscious one. Girard calls the identification and lynching of a victim the "single victim mechanism." This mechanism or operation is the community's unconscious way of converging upon someone it blames for its troubles. When this happens, the community actually believes the accusation it makes against the unfortunate person. One way to put this, in the language of the Bible, especially the Gospels, is that this entire single victim process is the work of Satan. Indeed, it *is* Satan.

4. *What or who is Satan, and how is he related to scandal?*

Answer: Satan or the devil, which are interchangeable titles in the New Testament, is the "accuser," the power of accusation and the power of the process resulting in blaming and eliminating a substitute for the real cause of the community's troubles. That real cause is the contagion of mimetic desire, which triggers the need for release from disorder, and this need in turn triggers the identification of a victim, someone who is weak or in some way marginal enough that the community can eliminate him or her without fear of reprisal. Satan as the "prince" or "first one" of this world is the "principle" or "first thing" of both order and disorder: of disorder because he is a figure representing rivalry and scandal, of order because he represents the mechanism that is triggered at the height of the disorder. "Satan casts out Satan" at this moment *in extremis,* just before the community explodes.

Satan has no real being; he exists always as a parasite on the being of humankind, just as theology tells us that he exists as a parasite on the being of God. Satan is imagined and symbolized as a person, as "someone," because satanic power becomes attached to the victim as the victim mechanism does its work. The victim is viewed as a devil or demon.

Satan and scandal thus overlap, but scandal describes primarily the process of desiring, then stumbling over models who are rivals and obstacles, and finally assigning blame, which leads to victimization. Satan describes primarily the mechanism of accusing and lynching a victim. Satan and scandal are key terms for understanding *mythology*.

5. *How is mythology related to Satan and scandal?*

Answer: Girard thinks comparing the various religions and their sacred stories is important. In fact, he calls the present study an essay in comparative religion. However, the comparative study of religion has typically missed the mark in two respects: (1) it has failed to notice that myths disguise real violence, and (2) it has usually reduced Christian origins to another myth because of similarities between Jesus' death and resurrection and the dying and rising of the gods in classical and ancient Near Eastern myths.

(1) Myths disguise real violence. Comparative scholars tend to miss this, or in some cases they simply may not want to see it. A great deal of the language and symbolism in myth is fantastic by rational and empirical criteria we ordinarily use in any kind of research or scientific work. Girard admits that much of myth is fantastic but holds that anthropologists and historians of religion have unfortunately held to a "one rotten apple spoils the whole barrel" approach. That is, because there *are* rotten apples, unbelievable things, in the stories and texts studied, then everything about them must be unbelievable. But this is not the case. There are still at least two good apples, and these are very important apples, indeed. One is evidence of real social crisis, violent contagion and disorder. This fact is joined by another: the crisis is ended by violence, specifically the lynching of a victim. The lynching is covered and disguised due to the belief that lies at the very origin of the myths: the victim really is the source of the troubles afflicting the community. Such belief results in transferring blame to the victim and exonerating the community. The myths always take the side of the community, the people, the crowd, against the one who is accused of criminal acts—a process well described in this book in the chapter on "The Horrible Miracle of Apollonius of Tyana."[1] (2) The similarities between the myths

---

1. For other analyses of myths, see Girard, *The Scapegoat* (Baltimore: Johns Hopkins University Press, 1986), chaps. 3, 5, 6; "Generative Scapegoating" in R. G. Hamerton-Kelly, ed., *Violent*

and the Gospel story of Jesus are real. To name the most obvious one: the god or hero dies and rises again. There is also a similarity between myths in which the central figure is dismembered and consumed and the Christian Eucharist, in which believers consume the body and blood of Christ. Girard argues, however, that the similarities serve essentially to point up the differences. The Passion account in the Gospels does not adopt the viewpoint of the crowd, of the authorities, even of the disciples of Jesus (unless it is the repentant disciples who later on, as they contribute to the Gospel accounts, don't try to hide their own shameful acts). It takes the side of the innocent victim, who gives himself over to God and lets himself suffer and die because of Satan's work, because of the victim mechanism, that those who believe in him may have their eyes and hearts opened and be saved. And those who henceforth "eat" his flesh and blood renounce any participation in killing the innocent victim and feast on the spiritual body of love and forgiveness he has offered them.

The various myths of humankind typically maintain the viewpoint and voice of the crowd, or the community, as it tries unawares to keep its victim mechanism in place. Myths are generally the narrative articulation of the basic human method of dealing with scandal. It is no wonder that Christian thought has perceived mythology as satanic and rejected it. In a sense, the gods of mythology are the product of Satan, of the working of accusation and the victim mechanism. Mythology is a justification of sacrifice for the sake of retribution and the victim mechanism. The Christian gospel is a proclamation of God's offering of himself to human beings in and through Jesus Christ. It is a different kind of sacrifice.

6. *What is the role of sacrifice in Girard's thought?*

Answer: The ritual act of sacrifice stems from the operation of the victim mechanism. The human or animal offered as a sacrifice is

---

Origins (Stanford: Stanford University Press, 1987), 73–105; and "Python and His Two Wives: An Exemplary Scapegoat Myth," in J. G. Williams, ed., *The Girard Reader* (New York: Crossroad, 1996), 118–41.

the victim par excellence. Human cultures begin with a spontaneous killing. As our prehuman ancestors developed a greater and greater brain capacity, with a greater and greater ability to imitate others and an accompanying loss of animal instincts, they often found themselves in confusion and trouble because of fear and panic. When frightened or threatened, whatever the cause, they imitated each other's reactions of fear. Sometimes this imitation was a reaction of striking out at someone in response to a blow (you hit me; I hit you—it can be an almost automatic, involuntary reaction). Imitation in the form of retaliation can destroy a group or community. But at some point various ancestors, converging upon someone among them—someone weak, or marginal (maybe an outsider)—came together again and gained relief from the stress of conflict and violence. They killed or expelled this person.

Indeed, we know that two kinds of practice or enactment emerged over time as the human ability to represent acts and thoughts became stronger. One was a ritual whose central act is the killing of a victim. Human victims were probably offered long before animal victims were substituted for humans. (Abraham's near sacrifice of Isaac in Genesis 22 is probably an allusion to this.)

The other practice is the ritual of expelling a victim. This could be called "scapegoating," a term based on the ritual described in Leviticus 16, which involves intentionally transferring the sins of the people onto a he-goat and driving the goat into the wilderness. But human beings were the victims in some settings, and this was probably the earlier practice. It is well documented, for example, that the ancient Greeks practiced a ritual requiring that one or more persons be selected, set aside for a period, beaten, and then murdered.

So sacrifice and scapegoating are two different expressions of the same reality, the victim mechanism by which human societies have typically operated. The mechanism is the origin of human culture, or "founding murder." A tremendous number of myths portray this founding murder, although the human reality is usually disguised and distorted. For example, in the ancient Babylonian myth of the origin of the world the god Marduk defeats Tiamat, the goddess of the salt water, splits her body, and places half of it over the sky and half under the earth. He kills Tiamat's consort, Kingu, and makes human beings out of his blood. This sounds like something that happened only in the realm of the gods, distant from human-kind. But what if the original victims were human and came to be known as gods? This is in fact what happened, according to Girard.

7. How is it that human beings became gods?

Answer: When a given group overcame its disorder and found new solidarity in community by eliminating someone among it, a victim, it experienced tremendous relief. There was peace; perhaps there was even a kind of euphoria for a while. Whether from just one experience of peace through slaying a victim or an accumulation of many such killings, the community's attention and dawning repre-sentational capacities become drawn more and more to the victim. If they could represent the victim as to blame, the one responsible for the troubles that befell them, then in a kind of metonymical reasoning process (one thing associated with another) it would ap-pear that the victim is also responsible for the new peace and order that have come about through the victim's death. And with peace and order, which means cooperation in the task of survival, there is greater prosperity.

Girard calls the transferring of blame onto the victim and then the transferring of credit for the new peace and prosperity "double transference." Now if the victim could cause all their troubles and yet also produce such peace and prosperity, he or she must be a different sort of being, a higher, more powerful sort. This is the birth of the gods. It was not a conscious process but began reflexively and developed and crystallized eventually into ritual representation of what had worked in the past. By the time the human ability to think critically had emerged in prophetic preaching or philosophical criticism, the origins of religion and culture were screened, covered, concealed, disguised. It's all there in the texts and other data, but not easy to spot.

As the victim dedicated for sacrifice became more important to human communities, the fact that the victim was "sacred," set aside to be offered up for the community, special attention was drawn to this designated person. Given the victim's inherent power in the community's eyes, if there was a delay between selection of the victim and the act of sacrifice, the victim would have had time to pull some people into his or her orbit. They became the victim's followers and wanted, not to sacrifice but to preserve the victim, at least for a much longer period of time. This, according to Girard, is the origin of kingship. Kings and queens have great power, but as those "far above" everyone else they are vulnerable. They can take credit for what goes right, but they can be blamed for what goes wrong. Either because of this vulnerability or their original victim status, or both, monarchs in primitive societies were often ritually slain, either periodically or occasionally. But in the biblical tradition, beginning with the Jewish Scriptures, there is a unique point of view on what is divine and what is human, on deity and victim.

8. *How is the Bible unique?*

Answer: The Bible is unique in its disclosure of the standpoint of the victim, which means that from the standpoint of the narratives, God takes the side of the victim. Not all narratives do this, but a new perspective emerges in Israel. What the people or crowd want is to justify itself and its past, and they do this by blaming someone for all their troubles. In moments of crisis caused by deep-seated rivalries a person is unjustly accused of some offense or crime. Or, as in the case of the Joseph story, the persecutors fear the person in question and are jealous of him. This is mimetic desire at work. The brothers of Joseph compete with him for the favor of their father, Jacob, but Jacob dotes on Joseph.

The brothers waylay Joseph and sell him into exile in Egypt. Later he is unjustly accused of rape by his Egyptian master's wife and thrown into prison. When Joseph finally gains prestige and power, he uses them to save Egypt and to save his family. Though his brothers expect him to retaliate by taking their lives, he forgives them and affirms the providence of God working through his sufferings.

God's siding with victims is especially prominent in the book of Psalms, which contains the first sustained outcries in world litera-ture of the single victim who is persecuted by enemies. This theme in the psalms is brought to a poetic crystallization in the sufferings of Job, who recognizes he is a scapegoat of the crowd and cries to God for help. And of course many of the prophets oppose sacrifice, connecting it to shedding of blood (Isa. 1:15; Hos. 6:6–8) and de-nouncing the offering of children as victims (Mic. 6:7; Jer. 32:35). The greatest prophetic figure of all, prior to Jesus, is the Servant of the Lord (Isa. 52:13–53:12), who is scapegoated by his people in Babylon and does not resist or protest. He is like a "lamb led to the slaughter," the Lamb of God.

So from a purely anthropological viewpoint, the Bible unveils the victim mechanism that lies behind polytheism and mythology, but not only behind polytheism and mythology, for its full expression underlies everything we know as human culture. The Bible recog-nizes this in the story of Cain and Abel. Because Cain murders his brother, God bans him from the soil, making him a wanderer on the earth, and God puts a mark on him, a sign to protect him from suffering what he made Abel suffer. Then Cain builds the first city, and so civilization begins. The story in Genesis 4 tells us, in ef-fect, that the sign of Cain is the sign of civilization. The cross of Christ is the sign of salvation, which is revealed as the overcoming of mimetic desire and violence through the nonviolence of love and forgiveness.

9. *How are the Gospels unique?*

Answer: The formal structure of the Gospels, as already men-tioned, is much like that of myth. A divine person, god or hero, is acclaimed, blamed for a crisis, put to death (usually by other divine beings), and rises again. The resurrection of the god or hero brings new blessings on the community, new peace and order. Though the structure of the Gospel story is very similar to that of myth, the similarity is not complete. One very important difference is that the community united around the one crucified and resurrected is a dissenting minority in both Jewish and Roman contexts. The Gospel story is not a myth uniting the entire social order.

But more important than structure is the perspective, the point of view, of the Gospel narratives. The chief figure, the one who teaches, dies, and rises again, is *innocent* of all the charges against him. All those around him desire something from him or something he prevents them from getting. The disciples want Jesus' approval and status in the new kingdom he proclaims. The crowds of people want healing and reassurance. The Jewish leaders are envious of his popularity and influence on the crowds that follow him. The Roman authorities desire order, the *pax Romana* or "Roman law and order." Jesus is an obstruction to that because he looks like a rabble-rouser: crowds follow him, there is talk that some want to acclaim him as the king of the Jews, and he causes a disturbance in the Temple, which frightens both the Roman governor and the Jewish priests.

So finally, all turn against him. It is the old mimetic scapegoating situation of all against one. Even his disciples turn against Jesus. One betrays him, another denies he is one of Jesus' followers, and all the others desert him. So Jesus, now alone and isolated, is put to death by the horrible Roman form of torture and execution—crucifixion.

But the disciples encounter Jesus as risen from the dead, and this encounter amounts to a true conversion, particularly as narrated in Luke and Acts. The mythic power of the victim mechanism is now subverted in principle. As human history continues, this satanic mechanism will be subverted more and more. The New Testament Gospels are the starting point for a new science or knowledge of humanity. This new knowledge begins with faith in Christ the innocent victim, and it becomes the leaven that will work itself out and expand to the point that the concern for victims becomes the absolute value in all societies molded or affected by the spread of Christianity.

10. What is the basis for saying that the concern for victims is the new absolute value?

Answer: The historical basis, first of all, is the revelation of God in Jesus Christ that the Gospels and the early oral tradition attest. The Jewish Scriptures, the Law and the Prophets, had already witnessed that God opposes idolatry and stands on the side of the oppressed and those who are unjustly accused of crimes. Two good examples of the narrative witness to the God who comes to the aid of victims are the Joseph story and the account of the Exodus from Egypt. In the Joseph story God works behind the scenes, and Joseph, the "master of dreams," interprets the story of his family and his sufferings and successes in Egypt as the providential guidance of God. In the exodus story God comes to the rescue of an oppressed people through a marginal figure, Moses. Moses is "marginal" in that he is a Hebrew but was raised as an Egyptian and comes from a slave class but has become identified with the Egyptian ruling class. He flees from Egypt because he kills an Egyptian mistreating a Hebrew, and he marries a Midianite woman. We can understand why the Hebrews mistrust him at first. But God speaks to him at the burning bush at Mt. Horeb: "I have witnessed the affliction of my people in Egypt and have heard their cry of complaint against their slave drivers, so I know well what they are suffering" (Exod. 3:7).

In the Gospels the revelation of the innocent victim revolves around Jesus' word and Jesus as the Word. Jesus' word, his message, focuses on God's plan to establish a community of love and joy— the "kingdom of God"—in which the values and distinctions and concern for power, prestige, and possessions in the ordinary world of mimetic rivalries and scandals will be overturned. The first will be last. Blessed are the meek, says Jesus, those who renounce retaliation and serve the heavenly Father who makes his sun rise on those accounted "good" and those considered "bad." God the Father takes care of all his creatures. Like a good shepherd he seeks even a single sheep that is lost.

Jesus as the Word is the exemplar of his teaching: he seeks and speaks to those who are lost, helpless, hungry, sick. The first disciples know he is the Word, the Son of God, only when he is expelled from the ordinary world of mimetic desire and rivalry. Jesus could have been viewed as just one more innocent victim crushed by some system of religious and political beliefs. The disciples might have felt sorry for him, felt guilty about deserting him, but what could they do? They themselves were naturally part of the world of jockeying for power and prestige and possessions. Even if they are willing to give up all they possess (Mark 10:28), they still desire the power and prestige of being associated with a great ruler in a new age (Mark 10:35–45). All the models they have unconsciously patterned themselves after have taught them they must gain some advantage or profit from the commitment to the kingdom.

Only when the disciples know that the innocent victim is not simply like all the other thousands and millions who have been tortured and expelled and killed since the foundation of the world, only when they experience him as the Risen One and confirm that he is indeed Lord and Messiah, the Son of God, is a new religious vision and a new set of values fully born in human history. What began like a mustard seed or bit of leaven now begins to move in human history from its Jewish beginnings into the whole world.

Friedrich Nietzsche knew this. He cast off the Christian faith of his Lutheran ancestors, but he recognized that a new perspective on the world and a new kind of religious personality were born in the traditions and Scriptures of the Jewish people and came to fruition in the teachings of Jesus and the way in which his followers perceived his death. Nietzsche would have none of it. He maintained a certain admiration for Jesus as a molder of human minds and hearts, but he detested the Jewish-Christian "slave morality," the ethics of affirming the worth and dignity of every person, no matter how lowly. He despised the idea of the equality of all souls before God. Nietzsche reaffirmed pagan virtues, especially from ancient Greek culture, and he held that for the human race to evolve toward the "Overman" (beginning with him and his poetic creation, Zarathustra) people must be willing to sacrifice human lives that stand in the way of this. He did not mean offering them in sacrifice on an altar, but sweeping aside the weak who were unable to contribute to creating new traditions and institutions and waging war.

For Girard, Nietzsche is very important as a great philosopher who saw quite clearly the new absolute value that Christianity had injected into Western culture. He acutely perceived that it was associated with democracy, a political form he held in contempt. This absolute value—concern for the victim—was already becoming secularized, torn from its religious and theological moorings, in Nietzsche's time. But an absolute value is not proven by logic or metaphysical arguments; it is accepted, believed (even when not discussed), and hedged about with taboos to protect it.

One of the proofs that the concern for victims is the absolute value of the modern Western world, and the absolute value wherever Western influence has had a deep impact, is a negative one: Nietzsche's interpreters avoid the subject. They circumvent Nietzsche's actual position on this subject. They revere Nietzsche; they look to him as the source of wisdom and his writings as a kind of holy scripture. However, it is extremely rare to find a "postmodern" follower of Nietzsche who raises a question about the very thing that Nietzsche railed against: the concern for victims that stems from Judaism and Christianity.[2]

The concern for victims has become such an absolute value that not only do those Nietzsche influenced not attack it, but it has become the unspoken dogma of "political correctness" and "victimism." Political correctness surrounds most of our public institutions, including above all colleges and universities, with an aura that prohibits using any word or allowing any discussion that might offend some minority group or victim or potential victim. It tends to stifle public discussion and debate of ideas and issues. Victimism uses the ideology of concern for victims to gain political or economic

---

2. An exception is Martin Heidegger, who fully realized what was at stake and who consciously and deliberately tried to expel the Jewish and Christian revelation from his own thinking and view of culture and the state. We can see this clearly not only in his writings but also in his commitment to the Nazi party. But likewise in the case of Heidegger his followers tend not to raise questions about the new absolute, the concern for victims.

or spiritual power. One claims victim status as a way of gaining an advantage or justifying one's behavior.

Both political correctness and victimism stem from an authentic reality from the standpoint of the Christian faith. That reality is God's revelation through Jesus Christ of the victim mechanism and the way into God's new community of love and nonviolence. But Satan has a tremendous ability to adapt to what God does and to imitate God, and so Satan—the ancient and tremendous power of the victim mechanism that expels violence through violence—is able to disguise himself and pose even as concern for victims.

But even if Christ has not yet completely overcome Satan in this world, more and more light is shed on his greed for victims because of our new awareness of scapegoating and our attempts to avoid victimization. Even if we often overreact and develop dogmas and practices that contradict the concern for victims, the work of the Cross continues in history. As St. Paul says:

> The word of the Cross is foolishness to those who are perishing, but to us who are being saved it is the power of God. For it is written:
>
> > "I will destroy the wisdom of the wise,
> > and the learning of the learned I will set aside."
>
> Where is the wise person? Where is the scribe? Where is the debater of this age? Has not God made the wisdom of the world foolish? . . . Jews demand signs and Greeks look for wisdom, but we proclaim Christ crucified, a stumbling block to Jews and foolishness to Gentiles, but to those who are called, Jews and Greeks alike, Christ the power of God and the wisdom of God.
>
> > (1 Cor. 1:18–20, 22–24)

JAMES G. WILLIAMS

Translator's Acknowledgments

I would like to thank my friend Rusty Palmer for his help in improving this translation. He read all the chapters and made numerous valuable comments and suggestions. Any mistakes or lack of clarity are, of course, my own responsibility.

I have usually followed the New American Bible where biblical passages are quoted. I have modified the renderings, however, for the sake of accuracy and nuances of meaning in context.

Introduction

To most of us, it goes without saying that the similarities between mythology and the Gospels play into the hands of religious relativists. That is why Christians have always denied or minimized their importance, with disastrous results. I argue that these similarities should be boldly explored. Far from threatening Christian uniqueness, they provide the sole basis upon which it can be made obvious, unquestionable.

How can this be? All mythical and biblical dramas, including the Passion, represent the same type of collective violence against a single victim. Myths see this victim as guilty: Oedipus has really killed his father and married his mother. The Bible and Gospels see these same victims as innocent, unjustly murdered by deluded lynchers and persecutors. Jesus is the unjustifiably sacrificed *lamb of God*.

All such victims are what we now familiarly call "scapegoats," innocent targets of a senseless collective transference that is mimetic and mechanical. Myths go along with this charade, but the Bible and the Gospels do not. Far from surrendering to some "morality of the slaves," as Nietzsche claimed, the biblical tradition punctures a universal delusion and reveals a truth never revealed before, the innocence not only of Jesus but of all similar victims.

As soon as we detect the concealed scapegoating behind mythology, all recurrent features of mythical heroes make sense: their frequent physical blemishes and their foreign identities—Oedipus limps; he comes from Corinth—and also the other features that are known to polarize angry mobs against their possessors. All these features must be as real as the "crimes" of these same victims are

1

imaginary. Being unanimous against their scapegoats, archaic mobs are appeased and reconciled by their death. This reconciliation explains why these scapegoats are divinized as both culprits and saviors, as the simultaneously good and bad divinities of the archaic sacred.

The concealed scapegoat hypothesis illuminates not only mythology but blood sacrifices, which deliberately reenact the original scapegoating and are done as a precaution against a possible relapse into violence. The various pieces of archaic religion fall into place like the pieces of a puzzle, a great many puzzles.

What I propose illuminates the divergences as well as the convergences between the biblical and the mythical, not merely the innocence of the victims versus their guilt, but the fact that, in mythology, no one ever questions this guilt. In the Gospels, the revealing account of scapegoating emanates not from the unanimous crowd but from a dissenting few. Initially, Jesus' disciples almost surrender to the mimetic power of the many, but on the third day, thanks to the Resurrection, they secede from the deluded mob and proclaim the innocence of their Lord. In mythology no dissenting voice is ever heard.

Many neglected themes in the Gospels come back to life, such as the "powers and principalities" and also Satan. We can understand why the prince of darkness is, among other things, the misleading *accuser* of innocent victims. We can also answer the famous question *How can Satan expel Satan?* The prince of this world is both the violence that he must expel in order to perpetuate his kingdom and the mechanism that does the expelling, which is no more than one particular modality of mob violence.

Jesus is not divinized by the false unanimity that puts only a temporary end to collective violence. He is an unsuccessful scapegoat whose heroic willingness to die for the truth will ultimately make the entire cycle of satanic violence visible to all people and therefore inoperative. The "kingdom of Satan" will give way to the "kingdom of God."

Thanks to Jesus' death, the Spirit of God, alias the *Paraclete* (a word that signifies "the lawyer for the defense"), wins a foothold in the kingdom of Satan. He reveals the innocence of Jesus to the disciples first and then to all of us. The defense of victims is both a moral imperative and the source of our increasing power to demystify scapegoating.

The Passion accounts reveal a phenomenon that unbeknownst to us generates all human cultures and still warps our human vision in favor of all sorts of exclusions and scapegoating. If this analysis is true, the explanatory power of Jesus' death is much greater than we realize, and Paul's exalted idea of the Cross as the source of all knowledge is anthropologically sound.

The opposition between the scapegoat concealed in mythology and unconcealed in Judaism and Christianity illuminates not only archaic religions, not only many neglected features of the Gospels, but above all the relationship between the two, the unique truth of the Judeo-Christian tradition. Since all this knowledge comes from the Gospels, the present book can define itself as a defense of our Judaic and Christian tradition, as an *apology* of Christianity rooted in what amounts to a Gospel-inspired breakthrough in the field of social science, not of theology.

Since this book vindicates the intellectual power of the Bible and Gospels, it can only increase our confidence in our religious tradition, which is an essential component of religious faith. This consequence is only indirect, however. At no point do I attempt to demonstrate the undemonstrable, the scientific truth of our religious faith.

apologetics

Part One

The Biblical Knowledge
of Violence

Chapter 1

Scandal Must Come

In the Bible, and especially in the Gospels, there is an original conception of desire and its conflicts that has gone largely unrecognized. In order to grasp how old it is we must go back to the Fall in Genesis or to the second half of the Ten Commandments, which is entirely devoted to prohibiting violence against one's neighbor.

Commandments six, seven, eight, and nine are both simple and brief. They prohibit the most serious acts of violence in the order of their seriousness:

> You shall not kill.
> You shall not commit adultery.
> You shall not steal.
> You shall not bear false witness against your neighbor.

The tenth and last commandment is distinguished from those preceding it both by its length and its object: in place of prohibiting an *act* it forbids a *desire*.

> You shall not covet the house of your neighbor. You shall not covet the wife of your neighbor, nor his male or female slave, nor his ox or ass, nor anything that belongs to him.
>
> (Exod. 20:17)

Without being actually wrong the modern translations lead readers down a false trail. The verb "covet" suggests that an uncommon desire is prohibited, a perverse desire reserved for hardened sinners. But the Hebrew term translated as "covet" means just simply "desire." This is the word that designates the desire of Eve for the prohibited fruit, the desire leading to the original sin. The notion

7

that the Decalogue devotes its supreme commandment, the longest of all, to the prohibition of a marginal desire reserved for a minority is hardly likely. The desire prohibited by the tenth commandment must be the desire of all human beings—in other words, simply desire as such.

If the Decalogue forbids the most widespread desire, doesn't it then deserve the modern world's reproach to religious prohibitions? Doesn't the tenth commandment succumb to that gratuitous itch to prohibit, to that irrational hatred of freedom for which modern thinkers blame religion in general and the Judeo-Christian tradition in particular?

Before condemning prohibitions as needlessly repressive, before espousing the formula rendered famous by the events of May 1968 in France—"Il est interdit d'interdire" [It is forbidden to forbid]— we must pose some questions about the implications of desire as it is defined in the tenth commandment, the desire for the neighbor's goods. If this desire is the most common of all, what would happen if it were permitted rather than forbidden? There would be perpetual war in the midst of all human groups, subgroups, and families. The door would be wide open to the famous nightmare of Thomas Hobbes, *the war of all against all.*

If we think that cultural prohibitions are needless, we must adhere to the most excessive individualism, one that presupposes the total autonomy of individuals, that is, *the autonomy of their desires.* In other words, we must think that humans are naturally inclined *not* to desire the goods of their neighbors. To understand that this premise is false, all we have to do is to watch two children or two adults who quarrel over some trifle. It is the opposite premise, the only realistic one, that underlies the tenth commandment of the Decalogue: we tend to desire what our neighbor has or what our neighbor desires.

If individuals are naturally inclined to desire what their neighbors possess, or to desire what their neighbors even simply desire, this means that rivalry exists at the very heart of human social relations. This rivalry, if not thwarted, would permanently endanger the

Reciprocal escalation
Decalogue - fundamental
new insight

harmony and even the survival of all human communities. Rivalistic desires are all the more overwhelming since they reinforce one another. The principle of reciprocal escalation and one-upmanship governs this type of conflict. This phenomenon is so common, so well known to us, and so contrary to our concept of ourselves, thus so humiliating, that we prefer to remove it from consciousness and act as if it did not exist. But all the while we know it does exist. This indifference to the threat of runaway conflict is a luxury that small ancient societies could not afford.

The commandment that prohibits desiring the goods of one's neighbor attempts to resolve the number one problem of every human community: internal violence.

IN READING THE TENTH COMMANDMENT one has the impression of being present at the intellectual process of its elaboration. To prevent people from fighting, the lawgiver seeks at first to forbid all the objects about which they ceaselessly fight, and he decides to make a list of these. However, he quickly perceives that the objects are too numerous: he cannot enumerate all of them. So he interrupts himself in the process, gives up focusing on the objects that keep changing anyway, and he turns to what never changes. Or rather, he turns to that one who is always present, the neighbor. One always desires *whatever belongs to that one,* the neighbor.

Since the objects we should not desire and nevertheless do desire always belong to the neighbor, it is clearly the neighbor who renders them desirable. In the formulation of the prohibition, the neighbor must take the place of the objects, and indeed he does take their place in the last phrase of the sentence that prohibits no longer objects enumerated one by one but "anything that belongs to him [the neighbor]." What the tenth commandment sketches, without defining it explicitly, is a fundamental revolution in the understanding of desire. We assume that desire is objective or subjective, but in reality it rests on a third party who gives value to the objects. This third party is usually the one who is closest, the neighbor. To maintain peace between human beings, it is essential to define pro-

Imitation / opposition

hibitions in light of this extremely significant fact: our neighbor is the model for our desires. This is what I call mimetic desire.[1]

MIMETIC DESIRE does not always result in conflict, but it frequently does so for reasons that the tenth commandment makes evident. The object I desire in envious imitation of my neighbor is one he intends to keep for himself, to reserve for her own use; she will not let someone snatch it away without combat. My desire will be thwarted, but in place of accepting this and moving on toward another object, nine times out of ten my desire will resist this and become even more intense in imitating the desire of its model.

Opposition exasperates desire, especially when it comes from the man or woman who inspires the desire. If no opposition initially comes from him or her, it soon will, for if imitation of the neighbor's desire engenders rivalry, rivalry in turn engenders imitation. The appearance of a rival seems to validate the desire, the immense value of the object desired. Imitation becomes intensified at the heart of the hostility, but the rivals do all they can to conceal from each other and from themselves the cause of this intensification. Unfortunately, concealment doesn't work. In imitating my rival's desire I give him the impression that he has good reasons to desire what he desires, to possess what he possesses, and so the intensity of his desire keeps increasing.

As a general rule, quiet and untroubled possession weakens desire. In giving my model a rival I return to him, in a way, the gift of the desire that he just gave to me. I give a model to my own model. The spectacle of my desire reinforces his at the precise moment when, in confronting me, he reinforces mine. That man whose wife I desire, for example, had perhaps ceased to desire her over time. His desire was dead, but upon contact with mine, which is living, it regains life. The mimetic nature of desire accounts for the fragility of human

---

1. "Mimesis" or "mimetic desire" is the most important concept for understanding Girard's thought. It is what lies behind the rivalistic conflict that leads to scapegoating. One may translate it as "imitation" or "imitative desire." However, he thinks that "mimetic" serves to highlight the conflictive aspect of imitation in a way that "imitation" does not. — Trans.

Blind spot of social anthropology
Individualism — self-idolization
Love neighbor as oneself

relations. Our social sciences should give due consideration to a phenomenon that must be considered *normal,* but they persist in seeing conflict as something accidental, and consequently so unfore-seeable that researchers cannot and must not take it into account in their study of culture. Not only are we blind to the mimetic rivalries in our world, but each time that we celebrate the power of our desire we glorify it. We congratulate ourselves on having within us a desire that "will last forever," as Baudelaire put it ("l'expansion des choses infinies"), but we do not see what this "forever" conceals: the idol-ization of the neighbor. This idolatry is necessarily associated with the idolization of ourselves. The more desperately we seek to worship ourselves and to be good "individualists," the more compelled we are to worship our rivals in a cult that turns to hatred.

The conflicts resulting from this double idolatry of self and other are the principal source of human violence. When we are devoted to adoring our neighbor, this adoration can easily turn to hatred be-cause we seek desperately to adore ourselves, and we fall. In order to prevent all such predicaments, the book of Leviticus contains the famous commandment "You shall love your neighbor *as yourself*" (Lev. 19:18); that is, you shall love your neighbor neither more nor less than yourself. The rivalries of desires tend to become exasper-ated, and as they do, they tend to contaminate third parties who are just as addicted as we are to the entanglements of mimetic rivalries.

cf. also "Golden Rule"

The principal source of violence between human beings is mi-metic rivalry, the rivalry resulting from imitation of a model who becomes a rival or of a rival who becomes a model. Such conflicts are not accidental, but neither are they the fruit of an instinct of aggression or an aggressive drive. Mimetic rivalries can become so intense that the rivals denigrate each other, steal the other's pos-sessions, seduce the other's spouse, and, finally, they even go as far as murder.

I have just mentioned again, though this time in reverse order, the four major acts of violence prohibited by the four commandments that precede the tenth. These are the ones I have already quoted at the beginning of this chapter. If the Decalogue devotes its final

Conflict engenders

commandment to prohibiting desire for whatever belongs to the neighbor, it is because it lucidly recognizes in that desire the key to the violence prohibited in the four commandments that precede it. If we ceased to desire the goods of our neighbor, we would never commit murder or adultery or theft or false witness. If we respected the tenth commandment, the four commandments that precede it would be superfluous.

of Paul in Rom 7:7-8

Rather than beginning with the cause and pursuing then the consequences, like a philosophical account, the Decalogue follows the reverse order, tackling the most urgent matter first: in order to avoid violence it forbids violent acts. It turns then to the cause and uncovers the desire that the neighbor inspires. The Decalogue prohibits this desire but is able to prohibit it only to the extent that the objects desired are legally possessed by one of the two rivals. It cannot discourage *all* the rivalries of desire.

IF WE EXAMINE the prohibitions of archaic societies in the light of the tenth commandment, we find that although they are not as lucid as the latter, they attempt likewise to prohibit mimetic desire and its rivalries. The prohibitions that appear arbitrary stem neither from some sort of "neurosis" nor from the resentment of grumpy men eager to prevent young people from having a good time. The prohibitions have nothing of the capricious or the mean about them; they are based on an intuition analogous to that of the Decalogue, but they are subject to all sorts of confusions.

Many archaic laws, notably in Africa, put to death all twins who are born in the community, or sometimes only one twin of each pair. Without doubt this law is absurd, but in no way does it prove the truth of cultural relativism. The cultures that do not tolerate twins confuse their natural resemblance in the biological order with the leveling effects of mimetic rivalries. The more these rivalries are aggravated, the more the roles of model, obstacle, and imitator become interchangeable at the heart of the mimetic conflict.

In short, to the extent that their antagonism becomes embittered, a paradox occurs: the antagonists resemble one another more and *milarity.*

True idea of imitating Christ

Imago Dei

more. They confront one another all the more implacably because their conflict dissolves the real differences that formerly separated them. Envy, jealousy, and hate render alike those they possess, but in our world people tend to misunderstand or ignore the resemblances and identities that these passions generate. They have ears only for the deceptive celebration of differences, which rages more than ever in our societies, not because real differences are increasing but because they are disappearing.

THE TENTH COMMANDMENT signals a revolution and prepares the way for it. This revolution comes to fruition in the New Testament. If Jesus never speaks in terms of prohibitions and always in terms of models and imitation, it is because he draws out the full conse-quences of the lesson offered by the tenth commandment. It is not due to inflated self-love that he asks us to imitate him; it is to turn us away from mimetic rivalries.

What is the basis of imitating Jesus? It cannot be his ways of being or his personal habits: imitation is never about that in the *not even prayer?* Gospels. Neither does Jesus propose an ascetic rule of life in the sense of Thomas à Kempis and his celebrated *Imitation of Christ,* as admirable as that work may be. What Jesus invites us to imitate is his own *desire,* the spirit that directs him toward the goal on which his intention is fixed: to resemble God the Father as much as possible.

The invitation to imitate the desire of Jesus may seem paradoxi-cal, for Jesus does not claim to possess a desire proper, a desire "of his very own." Contrary to what we ourselves claim, he does not claim to "be himself"; he does not flatter himself that he obeys only his own desire. His goal is to become the perfect *image* of God. There-fore he commits all his powers to imitating his Father. In inviting us to imitate him, he invites us to imitate his own imitation.

Far from being a paradox, this invitation is more reasonable than that of our modern gurus, who ask their disciples to imitate them as the great man or woman who imitates no one. Jesus, by contrast, invites us to do what he himself does, to become like him a perfect imitator of God the Father.

Detached generosity of God
How Jesus fulfills the Law
True + false freedom ——→

Rom 7:7

Why does Jesus regard the Father and himself as the best model for all humans? Because neither the Father nor the Son desires greedily, egotistically. God "makes his sun rise on the evil and on the good, and he sends his rain on the just and on the unjust." God gives to us without counting, without marking the least difference between us. He lets the weeds grow with the wheat until the time of harvest. If we imitate the detached generosity of God, then the trap of mimetic rivalries will never close over us. This is why Jesus says also, "Ask, and it will be given to you. . . ."

When Jesus declares that he does not abolish the Law but fulfills it, he articulates a logical consequence of his teaching. The goal of the Law is peace among humankind. Jesus never scorns the Law, even when it takes the form of prohibitions. Unlike modern thinkers, he knows quite well that to avoid conflicts, it is necessary to begin with prohibitions.

The disadvantage of the prohibitions, however, is that they don't finally play their role in a satisfying manner. Their primarily negative character, as St. Paul well understood, inevitably provokes in us the mimetic urge to transgress them. The best way of preventing violence does not consist in forbidding objects, or even rivalistic desire, as the tenth commandment does, but in offering to people the model that will protect them from mimetic rivalries rather than involving them in these rivalries.

Often we believe we are imitating the true God, but we are really imitating only false models of the independent self that cannot be wounded or defeated. Far from making ourselves independent and autonomous, we give ourselves over to never ending rivalries.

The commandment to imitate Jesus does not appear suddenly in a world exempt from imitation; rather it is addressed to everyone that mimetic rivalry has affected. Non-Christians imagine that to be converted they must renounce an autonomy that all people possess naturally, a freedom and independence that Jesus would like to take away from them. In reality, once we imitate Jesus, we discover that our aspiration to autonomy has always made us bow down before individuals who may not be worse than we are but who are none-

Mimetic desire intrinsically good
(rises above instinct)/

theless bad models because we cannot imitate them without falling with them into the trap of rivalries in which we are ensnarled more and more.

We feel that we are at the point of attaining autonomy as we imitate our models of power and prestige. This autonomy, however, is really nothing but a reflection of the illusions projected by our admiration for them. The more this admiration mimetically intensifies, the less aware it is of its own mimetic nature. The more "proud" and "egotistic" we are, the more enslaved we become to our mimetic models.

EVEN IF THE MIMETIC NATURE of human desire is responsible for most of the violent acts that distress us, we should not conclude that mimetic desire is bad in itself. If our desires were not mimetic, they would be forever fixed on predetermined objects; they would be a particular form of instinct. Human beings could no more change their desire than cows their appetite for grass. Without mimetic desire there would be neither freedom nor humanity. Mimetic desire is intrinsically good.

Humankind is that creature who lost a part of its animal instinct in order to gain access to "desire," as it is called. Once their natural needs are satisfied, humans desire intensely, but they don't know exactly what they desire, for no instinct guides them. We do not each have our own desire, one really our own. The essence of desire is to have no essential goal. Truly to desire, we must have recourse to people about us; we have to borrow their desires.

This borrowing occurs quite often without either the loaner or the borrower being aware of it. It is not only desire that one borrows from those whom one takes for models; it is a mass of behaviors, attitudes, things learned, prejudices, preferences, etc. And at the heart of these things the loan that places us most deeply into debt—the other's desire—occurs often unawares.

The only culture really ours is not that into which we are born; it is the culture whose models we imitate at the age when our power of mimetic assimilation is the greatest. If the desire of children were not mimetic, if they did not of necessity choose for models the human beings who surround them, humanity would have neither language nor culture. If desire were not mimetic, we would not be open to what is human or what is divine.

Mimetic desire enables us to escape from the animal realm. It is responsible for the best and the worst in us, for what lowers us below the animal level as well as what elevates us above it. Our unending discords are the ransom of our freedom.

IF MIMETIC RIVALRY plays an essential role in the Gospels, how does it happen, you may object, that Jesus does not put us on guard against it? Actually he does put us on guard, but we don't know it. When what he says contradicts our illusions, we ignore him.

The words that designate mimetic rivalry and its consequences are the noun *skandalon* and the verb *skandalizein*. Like the Hebrew word that it translates, "scandal" means, not one of those ordinary obstacles that we avoid easily after we run into it the first time, but a paradoxical obstacle that is almost impossible to avoid: the more this obstacle, or scandal, repels us, the more it attracts us. Those who are scandalized put all the more ardor in injuring themselves against it because they were injured there before.

The Greek word *skandalizein* comes from a verb that means "to limp." What does a lame person resemble? To someone following a person limping it appears that the person continually collides with his or her own shadow.

Understanding this strange phenomenon depends upon seeing in it what I have just described: the behavior of mimetic rivals who, as they mutually prevent each other from appropriating the object they covet, reinforce more and more their double desire, their desire for both the other's object of desire and for the desire of the other. Each consistently takes the opposite view of the other in order to escape their inexorable rivalry, but they always return to collide with the fascinating obstacle that each one has come to be for the other.

Scandals are responsible for the false infinity of mimetic rivalry. They secrete increasing quantities of envy, jealousy, resentment,

— an infernal prison.

hatred—all the poisons most harmful not only for the initial antagonists but also for all those who become fascinated by their rivalistic desires. At the height of scandal each reprisal calls forth a new one more violent than its predecessor. If nothing stops it, the spiral has to lead to a series of acts of vengeance in a perfect fusion of violence and contagion.[2]

"Woe to the one by whom scandal comes!" Jesus reserves his most solemn warning for the adults who seduce children into the infernal prison of scandal. The more the imitation is innocent and trusting, the more the one who imitates is easily scandalized, and the more the seducer is guilty of abusing this innocence. Scandals are so formidable that to put us on guard against them, Jesus resorts to an uncharacteristic hyperbolic style: "If your hand scandalizes you, cut it off; if you eye scandalizes you, pull it out" (Matt. 18:8–9).

Recent translators, trying to make the Bible psychoanalytically correct, attempt to eliminate all the terms censured by contemporary dogmatism. They replace the admirable "stumbling block" of our older Bibles, for example, with insipid euphemisms, although "stumbling block" is the only translation that captures the repetitive and addictive dimension of scandals.

Jesus would not be astonished that his teaching is not recognized. He has no illusion about the way in which his message will be received. To the glory that comes from God, invisible in this world, the majority prefer the glory that comes from humankind, a glory that multiplies scandal as it makes its way. It consists in gaining victory in mimetic rivalries often organized by the powers of this world, rivalries that are political, economic, athletic, sexual, artistic, intellectual ... and even religious.

The phrase "Scandal must come" (see Matt. 18:7) has nothing to do with either ancient fatalism or scientific determinism. Taken

---

2. Girard uses *mimétisme* here, for which English has no equivalent. In his usage it refers to imitation of others' desires and a complex of rivalries that spread rapidly and increase to the point that scandals begin to accumulate. This is an unconscious process that leads to the "war of all against all" if it were not for a mechanism, an unconscious operation, that avoids chaos by the unanimous resort to expelling or lynching a victim. In subsequent chapters I often translate *mimétisme* as "violent contagion." — Trans.

individually, human beings are not necessarily given over to mimetic rivalries, but by virtue of the great number of individuals they contain, human communities cannot escape them. When the first scandal occurs, it gives birth to others, and the result is *mimetic crises*, which spread without ceasing and become worse and worse.

Chapter 2

The Cycle of Mimetic Violence

THE CROWD is still favorable to Jesus when he enters Jerusalem, but it turns suddenly against him, and its hostility becomes so contagious that it spreads to the most diverse individuals. The theme that dominates the narratives of the Passion, especially in the first three Gospels, is the uniformity of reactions among those involved. These reactions stem from the prevailing power of the *peer* social body, or in other words mimetic contagion. In the Gospels all *pressure* themes lead to the Passion. Scandals play a role too important to escape from this law of convergence toward a single victim.

Peter is the most spectacular example of mimetic contagion. His love for Jesus is not in question; it is as sincere as it is profound. Yet as soon as the apostle is plunged into a crowd hostile to Jesus, he is unable to avoid imitating its hostility. If the first of the disciples, the rock on which the Church will be established, succumbs to the collective pressure, how will the others around Peter, just average people, be able to resist? To indicate that Peter will deny him, Jesus refers expressly to the role of scandal—mimetic conflict—in the apostle's life. The Gospels show him to be the puppet of his own mimetic desire, incapable of resisting pressures that work upon him from moment to moment.

Those who look for the causes of Peter's threefold denial only in the "temperament" of the apostle or in his "psychology" are on the wrong track, in my opinion. They do not see anything in the episode that goes beyond Peter as an individual. They believe, therefore, that they can make a "portrait" of the apostle. They attribute to him a "temperament particularly impressionable and impulsive," or owing to other formulas of the same kind, they destroy the typical

19 *but there is other evidence for this.*

character of the event and minimize its Christian significance. The main thing, I repeat, cannot be the psychology of the individual named Peter. In succumbing to the violent contagion that does not spare any of the witnesses of the Passion, Peter is not distinguished from any of the other disciples in a psychological sense.

Resorting to a psychological explanation is less innocent than it appears. In refusing the mimetic interpretation, in looking for the failure of Peter in purely individual causes, we attempt to demonstrate, unconsciously of course, that in Peter's place we would have responded differently; we would not have denied Jesus. Jesus reproaches the Pharisees for an older version of the same ploy when he sees them build tombs for the prophets that their fathers killed. The spectacular demonstrations of piety toward the victims of our predecessors frequently conceal a wish to justify ourselves at their expense: "If we had lived in the time of our fathers," the Pharisees say, "we would not have joined them in spilling the blood of the prophets."

The children repeat the crimes of their fathers precisely because they believe they are morally superior to them. This false difference is already the mimetic illusion of modern individualism, which represents the greatest resistance to the mimetic truth that is reenacted again and again in human relations. The paradox is that the resistance itself brings about the reenactment.

PILATE HIMSELF is also ruled by mimetic contagion. He would prefer to spare Jesus. If the Gospels insist upon this preference, it is not to suggest that the Romans are superior to the Jews, in other words: to allot good and bad points to the persecutors of Jesus. It is rather to underscore the paradox of the sovereign power that surrenders to the crowd and melts into it, as it were, for fear of an encounter with it. The account thus shows once again the omnipotence of mimetic contagion. What motivates Pilate, as he hands Jesus over, is the fear of a riot. He demonstrates "political skill," as they say. This is true, no doubt, but why does political skill almost always consist of giving in to violent contagion?

One of them is *(margin note)*

Even the two thieves crucified at either side of Jesus are no exception to universal contagion: they too imitate the crowd; like it they shout insults at Jesus. The most humiliated persons, the most crushed, behave in the same fashion as the princes of this world. They howl with the wolves. The more one is crucified, the more one burns to participate in the crucifixion of someone more crucified than oneself.

From the anthropological aspect the Cross is the moment when a thousand mimetic conflicts, a thousand scandals that crash violently into one another during the crisis, converge against Jesus alone. For the contagion that divides, fragments, and decomposes communities is substituted a collective contagion that gathers all those scandalized to act against a single victim who is promoted to the role of universal scandal. The Gospels try to draw our attention to the prodigious power of this contagion, but usually without success in the case of both Christians and their adversaries. This is difficult to perceive. In *The Joy of Being Wrong* James Alison calls the mimetic anthropology "transcendental," and what this recourse to the notion of transcendence suggests is the difficulty we all have in perceiving what is already revealed in the Gospels.

Is it necessary to refuse this mimetic anthropology in the name of a given theology? Is it necessary to see in the gathering against Jesus the work of God the Father, who like the divinities of the *Iliad* would move humankind to act against his Son in order to exact from him the ransom that they themselves could not provide? To me this interpretation appears contrary to both the spirit and the letter of the Gospels.

There is nothing in the Gospels to suggest that God causes the mob to come together against Jesus. Violent contagion is enough. Those responsible for the Passion are the human participants themselves, incapable of resisting the violent contagion that affects them all when a mimetic snowballing[1] comes within their range, or rather when they come within the range of this snowballing and are swept

---

1. The French phrase is *emballement mimétique*. *L'emballement* normally refers to excitement or an outburst of temper or enthusiasm. What Girard means is best captured by the vivid imagery

subtitle Original Sin —→ Easter Eyes (margin note)

along by it. We don't have to invoke the supernatural to explicate this. The war of *all against all* that transforms communities into a war of *all against one* that gathers and unifies them is not limited solely to the case of Jesus. We will soon see other examples of this.

To COMPREHEND WHY AND HOW the contagion that divides and frag-ments communities can be transformed suddenly into a contagion that gathers and reunites them against a single victim, we have to examine the way mimetic conflicts evolve. Beyond a certain thresh-old of frustration, those in conflict are no longer content with the objects themselves over which they are fighting. Mutually exasper-ated by the live obstacle, the scandal, that each is henceforth for the other, they become mimetic *doubles*[2] and forget the object of their quarrel; they turn against each other with rage in their heart. From now on each sets upon the other as a mimetic rival.

This type of rivalry does not destroy the reciprocity of human re-lations; rather it makes it more complete—in the sense of reprisals, of course, not of peaceful interaction. The more the antagonists desire to become different from each other, the more they become identical. Identity is realized in the hatred of the identical. This is the climactic moment that twins embody, or the enemy broth-ers of mythology such as Romulus and Remus. It is what I call a confrontation of *doubles*.

At first the antagonists occupy fixed positions at the heart of conflicts whose relentless character ensures stability, but as they persist, the interplay of scandals transforms them into a *mass* of interchangeable beings. In this homogeneous mass the mimetic im-pulses no longer encounter any obstacle and spread at high speed. This development favors the strangest about-faces and the most unexpected regroupings.

---

of the English "snowballing," whose primary meaning is a snowball's increase in speed and size as it rolls down a hill. —Trans.

2. "Mimetic doubles" refers to the situation in which rivals become so obsessed with each other that they mirror each other's emotions and actions. The doubles are alike but they mistak-enly see a great difference between them. Mimetic doubles are quite dangerous to one another and to others and can be quite self-destructive. —Trans.

Scandals initially appear rigid, immovably fixed on a specific antagonist, each forever separated from the other by reciprocal hatred, but at the advanced stages of this development substitutions come about as antagonists are exchanged. Then scandals become "opportunistic." At this point they are easily drawn to another scandal whose power of mimetic attraction is superior to theirs. In short, scandals may turn away from their original antagonist, from whom they seemed inseparable, in order to adopt the scandal of their neighbors and substitute a new antagonist for the original one.

What determines the scandal's power of attraction is the number and prestige of those it succeeds in scandalizing. Little scandals have a tendency to dissolve into larger ones, and the larger ones in turn go on to contaminate one another until the strongest of these absorb the weaker ones. There is a mimetic competition of scandals, which continues until the moment when the most polarizing scandal remains alone on the stage. This is when the whole community is mobilized against one and the same individual.

In the Passion, this individual is Jesus, which explains why Jesus resorts to the vocabulary of scandal to designate himself as everyone's victim and to designate all those who are polarized against him. He exclaims, "Happy is the one not scandalized by me." There will be throughout Christian history a tendency of Christians themselves to choose Jesus as an alternative scandal, that is, a tendency to lose themselves and merge into the mob of persecutors. For St. Paul, consequently, the Cross is the scandal par excellence. I would observe that the symbolism of the traditional cross, the crossing of the two branches, renders visible the internal contradiction of the scandal.

The disciples themselves are no exception to the common law of scandal. When Jesus becomes the universal scandal, they are all influenced, in varying degrees, by the universal hostility. This is why, a little before the Passion, Jesus speaks to them in the vocabulary of scandal, with a special warning to caution them about the failures that await them, to ease their remorse, perhaps, at the moment when they will understand the shame of their individual and collective abandonment of Jesus: "You will all be scandalized because of me."

Jesus' statement does not mean simply that the disciples will be troubled and afflicted by the Passion. When Jesus says something that seems banal, it is necessary to be wary. Here as elsewhere, we must give the word "scandal" its strong meaning, which is mimetic. Jesus warns his disciples they will all succumb more or less to the contagion that seizes the crowd, they will all participate to some extent in the Passion *on the side of the persecutors.*

Scandals between individuals are little streams that flow into the great rivers of collective violence. Or to use another metaphor, we can say that, like a swarm of bees around its queen, the scandals all swarm together around the single victim. The power that welds the scandals together is an intensified contagion. The word "scandal" gives the impression of being used haphazardly and to designate many different things, but in reality it always has to do with diverse moments of one and the same mimetic process, or with this process in its totality.

The more unbearable their personal scandals become, the more the desire to extinguish them in some huge scandal seizes the scandalized. This phenomenon can be seen quite clearly in political passions or in the frenzy of scandal that now possesses our "globalized" world. When a really seductive scandal comes near, the scandalized are irresistibly tempted to "profit" from it and to gravitate toward it. The condensation of all the separated scandals into a single scandal is the paroxysm of a process that begins with mimetic desire and its rivalries. These rivalries, as they multiply, create a mimetic crisis, the war of *all against all.* The resulting violence of all against all would finally annihilate the community if it were not transformed, in the end, into a war of *all against one,* thanks to which the unity of the community is reestablished.

THE VICTIM OF MIMETIC SNOWBALLING is chosen by the contagion itself; he or she is *substituted* for all the other victims that the crowd could have chosen if things had happened differently. Substitutions come about spontaneously, invisibly, as they take advantage of the sound and the fury signifying nothing (*Macbeth*). (In the case of Jesus, other factors entered in which keep us from seeing him as a victim of chance in the same sense as most of the victims of this type.)

Pilate is an administrator experienced enough to understand the role of substitutions in the case he is asked to settle. This is made clear to us by the famous episode of Barabbas. The Roman concern for legality suggests to Pilate that he had best not hand Jesus over; that is, it would be better if he did not give in to the crowd. Yet Pilate understands that this crowd will not be pacified without a victim. That is why he offers it a victim in compensation: he proposes to have Barabbas executed in exchange for Jesus. From Pilate's point of view Barabbas offers the advantage of being already legally condemned. His execution will not transgress the law. Pilate's principal concern is not to prevent the death of an innocent man, but to limit as much as possible the disorder that threatens to harm his reputation as an administrator in the higher imperial circles.

The fact that the crowd rejects Barabbas does not mean in any way that the Gospels accuse the Jewish people as a whole of harboring an undying, relentless hatred for Jesus. Long favorable to Jesus, then hesitant, the crowd is not completely hostile until the climax of the Passion. This variety of attitudes is quite characteristic of crowds in the throes of mimetic contagion. Once the unanimity comes about, the crowd seizes on the victim who emerges from the process, and it refuses exchange for another victim. The time for substitutions is over, and the moment of violence has sounded. Pilate comprehends this. When he sees that the crowd rejects Barabbas, he immediately hands over Jesus.

IF WE RECOGNIZE in the Crucifixion what is typical, even banal, we can then understand one of the themes of Jesus, which is the resemblance between his own death and the persecution of many prophets before him. Many people now think that if the Gospels report the death of Jesus as similar to that of the prophets, their goal is to stigmatize the Jewish people alone. This is of course what medieval anti-Semitism already imagined because it was based, like all Christian anti-Semitism, on an inability to understand the true nature and eminently typical character of the Passion. A thousand or more years ago, in an era when Christian influence had not profoundly penetrated our world, this error was more excusable than today.

The anti-Semitic interpretation fails to discern the real intention of the Gospels. It is clearly mimetic contagion that explains the hatred of the masses for exceptional persons, such as Jesus and all the prophets; it is not a matter of ethnic or religious identity. The Gospels suggest that a mimetic process of rejection exists in all communities and not only among the Jews. The prophets are the preferential victims of this process, a little like all *exceptional* persons, individuals who are *different.* The reasons for exceptional status are diverse. The victims can be those who limp, the disabled, the poor, the disadvantaged, individuals who are mentally retarded, and also great religious figures who are inspired, like Jesus or the Jewish prophets or now, in our day, great artists or thinkers. All peoples have a tendency to reject, under some pretext or another, the individuals who don't fit their conception of what is normal and acceptable. If we compare the Passion to the narratives of the violence suffered by the prophets, we confirm that in both cases the episodes of violence are definitely either directly collective in character or of collective inspiration. The *resemblance* of Jesus to the prophets is perfectly real, and we will soon see that these resemblances are not restricted to the victims of collective violence in the Bible. In myths as well, the victims are or seem *different.*

So it is necessary to interpret very concretely the statement of Jesus about the analogy between his own death and that of the prophets. To confirm the realistic interpretation that I propose, the Passion must be compared not only to the violence done to the Jewish prophets in the Old Testament but also to an event reported at length in the Gospels themselves, the execution of the one the Gospels regard as "the last of the prophets," John the Baptist.

IF JOHN THE BAPTIST is a prophet, then to conform to Jesus' teaching John's violent death must *resemble* the violent death of Jesus. That is, we should find in John's death the mimetic contagion and other essential features of the Passion. And indeed they are found there. We easily verify the presence of all the features in the two Gospels that narrate the death of John the Baptist. These are the two oldest ones, Mark and Matthew.

Just like the Crucifixion, the slaying of John the Baptist is not directly carried out by the crowd, but it is collectively inspired. In both cases there is a sovereign who is the only one with the authority to issue the decree of death and who finally decrees it in spite of his personal desire to spare the victim: Pilate on the one hand, Herod on the other. In both cases the ruler renounces his own desire and orders the execution of the victim for mimetic reasons, not being able to withstand a violent crowd. Just as Pilate does not dare confront the crowd that demands crucifixion, Herod does not dare confront his guests who demand the head of John.

In both cases everything stems from a mimetic crisis. Concerning the prophet, it is the crisis of the marriage of Herod to Herodias. John reproaches Herod for his illegal marriage to the wife of his brother; Herodias desires revenge but Herod protects John. To force his hand, at his birthday banquet Herodias stirs up the crowd of guests against her enemy. To whip up the mimetic contagion of this gathering and transform it into a bloody pack, Herodias resorts to the art that the Greeks took to be the most mimetic of all, the most apt at a sacrifice to motivate participants against the victim: dancing. Herodias has her own daughter dance. The dancer, manipulated by her mother, requests John's head as a reward, and the guests unanimously demand the head of John.

The resemblances between this narrative and the Passion are remarkable and cannot be attributed to a kind of plagiarism. The two texts are not "doublets" of each other. Their details are quite different. It is their internal mimetic character that renders them similar, and this is represented in a manner as powerful and original in one case as in the other.

At the anthropological level, therefore, the Passion is typical rather than unique: it illustrates the major event of the Gospel anthropology, namely, the victimary mechanism that appeases human communities and reestablishes, at least provisionally, their tranquility.

WHAT WE DISCOVER in the Gospels, in the death of Jesus as well as the death of John the Baptist, is a cyclic process of disorder and reestablishment of order that reaches its high point and ends in a mechanism of victimary unanimity. I am employing the word "mechanism" to signify the automatic nature of the process and its results, as well as the incomprehension and even the unconscious obedience of the participants. The most interesting biblical texts in relation to the victimary process are those that the Gospels themselves connect to the life and death of Jesus, those that recount the life and death of the figure named the Servant of Yahweh or the Suffering Servant.

The Servant is a great prophet who appears in the part of the book of Isaiah that begins at chapter 40, the part generally attributed to an independent author, Second Isaiah or Deutero-Isaiah. The passages evoking the life and death of this prophet are sufficiently distinct from those around them that they can be grouped into four separate sections that read like four grand poems, the songs of the Servant of Yahweh. Though the beginning of chapter 40, the first chapter of Second Isaiah, is not one of those, in certain respects I think it should be linked to them:

A voice cries:
"In the wilderness prepare the way of the LORD,
    make straight in the desert a highway for our God.
Every valley shall be lifted up,
    and every mountain and hill be made low;
the uneven ground shall become level,
    and the rough places a plain.
And the glory of the LORD shall be revealed,
    and all flesh shall see it together,
    for the mouth of the LORD has spoken." (Isa. 40:3–5, RSV)

In this leveling, this universal flattening, modern exegetes see an allusion to the construction of a route for Cyrus, the king of Persia, who permitted the Jews to return to Jerusalem. This explanation is certainly reasonable but a little flat. The text speaks of flattening—that is clear—but it does not speak about it flatly. It presents flattening as a subject so grand and impressive that to limit its scope to the construction of a great highway, even for the greatest of all monarchs, seems to me too narrow a view of it.

One of the themes of Second Isaiah is the end of the Babylonian Exile, which happily for the Jews was effected by the famous edict of Cyrus. But other themes are interwoven with that of the return, particularly the theme of the Servant of Yahweh. Rather than construction work undertaken with a predetermined goal, the text I quoted is reminiscent of a geological erosion, and I think it is necessary to see there an image of those mimetic crises whose essential feature is the loss of differences, the transformation of individuals into *doubles* whose perpetual conflict destroys culture. The text assimilates this process to the collapsing of mountains and the filling of valleys in a mountainous region. Just as the rocks are transformed into sand, so the people are transformed into an amorphous mass incapable of understanding "the voice crying in the wilderness," yet they are always ready to eat away at the heights and to fill up the depths in order to remain at the surface of all things, to reject greatness and truth.

As troubling as this leveling of differences may be, this overwhelming victory of the superficial and the uniform, the prophet invokes it because of the great transformation for which it paradoxically prepares the way, a decisive manifestation of Yahweh:

> And the glory of the LORD shall be revealed,
>   and all flesh shall see it together,
>   for the mouth of the LORD has spoken.

This epiphany here prophesied is evidently realized twelve chapters further on, in the collective murder that ends the crisis, the murder of the Suffering Servant. In spite of his kindness and his love for

others, the Servant is not loved by his own people, and in the fourth
and last song, he dies at the hands of a hysterical crowd that mobs
against him. He is the victim of a true lynching.

To understand Second Isaiah properly, I think it is necessary to
trace a great circular arc that emerges suddenly from the original
flattening, from the violent undifferentiation, and that comes down
in chapters 52 and 53 in the narrative of the violent death of the
Servant. This circular arc reconnects, in short, the description of
the mimetic crisis to the chief consequence of this crisis, the lynching of a single victim. This death, the murder of the great prophet
rejected by his people, is the equivalent of the Passion in the Gospels. As in the Gospels, the collective lynching of the prophet and
the revelation of Yahweh make up one and the same event.

Once we apprehend the structure of crisis and collective lynching
in Second Isaiah, we understand also that it constitutes, just as in
the life and death of Jesus in the Gospels, what I call a *mimetic
cycle*. The initial proliferation of scandals leads sooner or later into
an acute crisis at the climax of which unanimous violence is set off
against the single victim, the victim finally selected by the entire
community. This event reestablishes the former order or establishes
a new one out of the old. Then the new order itself is destined
someday to enter into crisis, and so on.

As in all mimetic cycles, the total sequence of events is a divine
epiphany, a manifestation of Yahweh. The mimetic cycle is represented in Second Isaiah with all the splendor characteristic of the
great prophetic texts. Like all mimetic cycles, this one resembles
those that precede and follow by its dynamism and its fundamental
structure. (At the same time, of course, it includes all sorts of features that belong only to it and that we need not enumerate.) The
proof that the same sequence is indeed found in the life and death
of Christ, as the four Gospel writers saw it, is that we encounter
in the four Gospels a description of the mimetic crisis that is literally the same as the description in Second Isaiah. This description
constitutes the heart of what John the Baptist prophesies concerning Jesus. To remind the audience of this chapter of Isaiah, to have

them think of that description of crisis and that announcement of the divine epiphany, is the same thing as prophesying Jesus: it is to announce that the life and death of Jesus will be *similar* to the life and death of the prophet of former times. It is to allude to what I call a new mimetic cycle, a new eruption of disorder culminating in the unanimous mimetic war of *all against one*.

John the Baptist is identified with "the voice crying in the wilderness," and his prophetic proclamation is entirely summarized in the quotation of chapter 40 of Isaiah. What the prophet intends to prophesy may be summarized as follows: "Once more we find ourselves in a great crisis, and it will end with the collective execution of a new envoy of God: Jesus. Yahweh will use his violent death as the occasion of a new and supreme revelation."

Chapter 3

Satan

anti-modern

Now I would like to confirm what I call the "mimetic cycle" in the Gospels. To do this we have to turn to an idea, or rather a figure, that Christians today much disdain. The Gospels call him by his Hebrew name, Satan, or his Greek title, the devil (*diabolos*).[1]

In the period when the German theologian Rudolf Bultmann had such great influence, all the theologians who were up to date "demythologized" the Scriptures with all their might, but they didn't even do the prince of this world the honor of demythologizing him. In spite of his considerable role in the Gospels, modern Christian theology scarcely takes him into account. If the Gospel references to Satan are examined in light of the preceding analyses, then we see that they don't deserve the oblivion into which they have fallen.

Like Jesus, Satan seeks to have others imitate him but not in the same fashion and not for the same reasons. He wants first of all to seduce. Satan as seducer is the only one of his roles that the modern world condescends to remember a bit, primarily to joke about it. Satan likewise presents himself as a model for our desires, and he is certainly easier to imitate than Christ, for he counsels us to abandon ourselves to all our inclinations in defiance of morality and its prohibitions.

If we listen to Satan, who may sound like a very progressive and likeable educator, we may feel initially that we are "liberated," but this impression does not last because Satan deprives us of everything that protects us from rivalistic imitation. Rather than warning us of

---

1. The synoptic Gospels use *satan/satanas* and *diabolos* interchangeably and with equal frequency. The Gospel of John uses *diabolos* three times and *satanas* one time. Both words refer to one who accuses, slanders, denounces, and seduces.

32

the trap that awaits us, Satan makes us fall into it. He applauds the idea that prohibitions are of no use and that transgressing them contains no danger.

The road on which Satan starts us is broad and easy; it is the superhighway of mimetic crisis. But then suddenly there appears an unexpected obstacle between us and the object of our desire, and to our consternation, just when we thought we had left Satan far behind us, it is he, or one of his surrogates, who shows up to block the route. This is the first of many transformations of Satan: the seducer of the beginnings is transformed quickly into a forbidding adversary, an opponent more serious than all the prohibitions not yet transgressed.

The secret of Satan's troublesome transformation is easy to discover. The second Satan is the conversion of the mimetic model into a rival, and this process, which was described in chapter 1, brings about scandals. Because our models suggest their own desires to us, they inevitably oppose the resulting desire. Once prohibitions are transgressed, another kind of obstacle rises up that is more tenacious still, though it is concealed at first by the very protection the prohibitions offer, as long as they are respected.

I am not the first or only one to relate Satan to scandals. The first was Jesus himself in a scathing rebuke to Peter: "Get behind me, Satan, for you are a scandal to me." Peter becomes the object of this rebuke when he reacts negatively to the first prediction of the Passion. Disappointed by what he takes to be the excessive resignation of Jesus, the disciple tries to breathe into him his own desire, his own worldly ambition. Peter invites Jesus, in short, to take Peter himself as the model of his desire. If Jesus were to turn away from his Father to follow Peter, he and Peter both would quickly fall into mimetic rivalry, and the venture of the kingdom of God would melt away in insignificant quarrels.

Here Peter becomes the sower of scandals, the Satan who diverts human beings from God for the sake of rivalistic models. Satan sows the scandals and reaps the whirlwind of mimetic crises. It is his opportunity to show what he is capable of doing. The great crises lead us to the true mystery of Satan, to his astonishing power, which is that of expelling himself and bringing order back into human communities.

The main text on the subject of the satanic expulsion of Satan is the response of Jesus to scribes who accuse him of expelling Satan by Beelzebub, the prince of demons:

> "How can Satan cast out Satan? If a kingdom is divided against itself, it cannot stand. And if a house is divided against itself, it cannot be maintained. And if Satan has risen up against himself and is divided, he cannot endure and is finished."
>
> (Mark 3:23–26)

Accusing a rival exorcist of expelling demons by the power of Satan must have been a common accusation in that period. Many people must have repeated it mechanically. Jesus wants to make his hearers reflect on its implications. If it is true that Satan expels Satan, how does he go about it? How is this tour de force possible?

Jesus does not deny the reality of Satan's self-expulsion; he asserts it. The proof that Satan possesses this power is the affirmation, frequently repeated, that this power is coming to its end. The imminent fall of Satan, prophesied by Christ, is one and the same thing as the end of his power of self-expulsion. The demonic or satanic expulsion of demons has worked previously, at least temporarily, because the violent outcome of scandal, the violent expulsion of scapegoats, works for a while.

In both Matthew and Mark, Jesus repeats the word "Satan" instead of replacing it with a pronoun. Jesus repeats the name: "How can Satan expel Satan?" Matthew changes the interrogative sentence of Mark into a conditional clause, but the basic formula does not change: "If Satan expels Satan." The repetition of the word "Satan" is more eloquent than its replacement by a pronoun, but it is not a taste for fine language that inspires it; it is rather the desire to emphasize the fundamental paradox of Satan. He is a principle of order as much as disorder.

The Satan expelled is that one who foments and exasperates mimetic rivalries to the point of transforming the community into a furnace of scandals. The Satan who expels is this same furnace when it reaches a point of incandescence sufficient to set off the single victim mechanism.[2] In order to prevent the destruction of his kingdom, Satan makes out of his disorder itself, at its highest heat, a means of expelling himself.

Because of this extraordinary power, Satan is the prince of this world. If he could not protect his domain from the violence that threatens to destroy it, even though it is essentially his own, he would not merit this title of prince, which the Gospels do not award him lightly. If he were purely a destroyer, Satan would have lost his domain long ago. To understand why he is the master of all the kingdoms of this world, we must take Jesus at his word: disorder *NOT WHAT JESUS SAYS* expels disorder, or in other words Satan really expels Satan. By executing this extraordinary feat, he has been able to make himself indispensable, and so his power remains great.

How do we comprehend this idea? Let us go back to the moment when the divided community, at the height of the mimetic process, reestablishes its unity against a single victim who becomes the supreme scandal because everyone, in a mimetic fervor, holds this one to be guilty. Satan is the violent contagion that persuades the entire community, which has become unanimous, that this guilt is real. He owes one of his most ancient and traditional names to this art of persuasion. He is the *accuser* of the hero in the book of Job, *Not in Job* before God and even more so before the people. In transforming a community of people with distinct identities and roles into a hysterical mass, Satan produces myths and is the principle of systematic accusation that bursts forth from the contagious imitation provoked by scandals. Once the unfortunate victim is completely isolated, deprived of defenders, nothing can protect her or him from the aroused

---

2. "Single victim mechanism" is a translation of the French *mécanisme victimaire*. It refers to the unconscious snowballing process that reaches a point of crisis and ends the disorder of human rivalries and scandals by expelling or lynching a victim. It could, of course, select more than one victim, perhaps a minority group, foreigners, et al., but for purposes of analysis and discussion Girard wishes to keep a clear focus on the simplest instance of the mechanism, which is also exemplary: convergence upon a single victim. — Trans.

crowd. Everyone can set upon the victim without having to fear the least reprisal. *But this does not happen in Job.*

The victim may seem insignificant in relation to all the appetites for violence that are converging on him or her, but at this very moment the community desires nothing other than the victim's destruction. This victim thus effectively replaces all those who were in conflict just a little earlier in the thousand scandals scattered here and there and who now are all mustered against a single target.

No one in the community has an enemy other than the victim, so once this person is hunted, expelled, and destroyed, the crowd finds itself emptied of hostility and without an enemy. Only one enemy was left, one who has been eliminated. Provisionally, at least, this community no longer experiences either hatred or resentment toward anyone or anything; it feels *purified* of all its tensions, of all its divisions, of everything fragmenting it.

The persecutors don't know that their sudden harmony, like their previous discord, is the work of contagious imitation. They believe they have on their hands a dangerous person, someone evil, of whom they must rid the community. What could be more sincere than their hatred? Thus the mimetic ganging up of *all against one*, or *the single victim mechanism*, has the amazing but logically explicable property of restoring calm to a community so disturbed an instant earlier that nothing appeared capable of calming it down.

To apprehend this mechanism as the work of Satan is to understand that what Jesus asserts—"Satan expels Satan"—has a precise meaning, rationally explainable. It defines the effectiveness of the single victim mechanism. The high priest Caiaphas alludes to this mechanism when he says, "It is better that one man die and that the whole nation not perish." The four accounts of the Crucifixion thus enable us to witness the unfolding of the working of the single victim mechanism. The sequence of events, as I have already said, resembles numerous analogous phenomena whose director and producer is Satan.

The proof that the Cross and the mechanism of Satan are one and the same thing is given by Jesus himself when he says just before his arrest, "This is your hour, and the power of darkness" (Luke 22:53). This hour, the moment of the power of darkness, is the hour of Satan. Jesus' statement is not a rhetorical formula, a picturesque way of suggesting the reprehensible character of what his persecutors are going to do to him. Like all the other Gospel statements on the subject of Satan, this one has a precise and even "technical" meaning. It is one of the statements that designate the Crucifixion as a working of the single victim mechanism.

The Crucifixion is one of those events in which Satan restores and consolidates his power over human beings. The shift from "all against all" to "all against one" permits the prince of this world to forestall the total destruction of his kingdom as he calms the anger of the crowd, restoring the calm that is indispensable to the survival of every human community. Satan can therefore always put enough order back into the world to prevent the total destruction of what he possesses without depriving himself for too long of his favorite pastime, which is to sow disorder, violence, and misfortune among his subjects.

The death of Jesus thwarts the satanic calculation. We will soon see why, but initially it does indeed have the effects that we would expect of the one who set it in motion. We can verify from the Gospels that Jesus' death has the pacifying effect that Pilate, just like Satan, expects of it. The outcome is quite favorable from the point of view of the *pax Romana,* of which Pilate is the guardian. The procurator feared a riot, but owing to the Crucifixion it did not occur.

The torture of a victim transforms the dangerous crowd into a public of ancient theater or of modern film, as captivated by the bloody spectacle as our contemporaries are by the horrors of Holly-wood. When the spectators are satiated with that violence that Aristotle calls "cathartic"—whether real or imaginary it matters little—they all return peaceably to their homes to sleep the sleep of the just.

The word "catharsis" designated first of all the "purification" that the spilled blood procures in ritual sacrifices, which are deliberate repetitions of the process described in the Passion. In other words it is the satanic mechanism at work. This mechanism is also presupposed in the phenomenon of exorcism, which is the subject in the debate that gives Jesus the occasion to raise the question about the satanic expulsion of Satan.

The Gospels enable us to see that human communities are subject to disorders that recur periodically and that can be resolved by the phenomenon of the *unanimous* crowd when certain conditions are satisfied. Such a resolution is rooted in mimetic desire and the scandals that always make human communities break down. The mimetic cycle begins with desire and its rivalries, it continues through the multiplication of scandals and a mimetic crisis, and it is resolved finally in the single victim mechanism, which is the answer to the question asked by Jesus: "How can Satan expel Satan?"

namely?   Certain medieval legends and traditional tales contain echoes of the Gospel concept of Satan. We see in these a kindly, generous man, always ready to lavish benefits on people for little in return, or so it seems. His only request is that one soul, only one, be reserved for him. Sometimes it is the daughter of the king whom he demands, but it doesn't really matter who it is. Anyone will do just as well as the most beautiful of princesses.

The demand appears modest, almost minute in comparison to the promised benefits, but the mysterious gentleman will not give it up. If it is not satisfied, all the gifts of the generous benefactor instantaneously vanish, and he vanishes with them. He is none other than Satan, of course, and to put him to flight it suffices not to give in to his blackmail. In this sort of tale there is a clear enough allusion to the prevailing power of the single victim mechanism in pagan societies and its perpetuation in veiled forms, often attenuated, in Christian societies.

ONE CAN SEE in all this an anthropology of mimetic desire, that is, an anthropology of crises that stem from mimetic rivalry and of crowd phenomena, which end these crises in triggering a new mimetic cycle. Such an anthropology is found in the Gospel of John.

In one of the discourses that he ascribes to Jesus, John inserts a short speech of fifteen verses. Though in it we find all that we analyzed in the synoptic Gospels, its form is so elliptical and condensed that it occasions even more misunderstanding than the Gospel statements that I have just examined. In spite of differences of vocabulary, which make it appear more difficult, the Johannine doctrine is the same as that of the synoptics.

Our contemporaries often condemn the text of John as superstitious and vindictive. What John does, however, is to define anew, abruptly indeed but also without hostility, the consequences for human beings of rivalistic imitation. In this discourse Jesus enters into dialogue with some people who will soon abandon him because they do not understand his teaching. Many of the first followers who listened to Jesus are already scandalized:

> "If God were your Father, you would love me,
> for I proceeded and came forth from God;
> I did not come forth of my own accord,
> but he himself sent me.
> Why don't you understand what I'm saying?
> It is because you are unable to hear my word.
> You are of your father the devil
> and it is the desires of your father
> that you wish to do.
> From the beginning he was a murderer
> and had nothing to do with the truth
> because the truth is not in him.
> When he speaks lies,
> he draws them from his own nature,
> because he is a liar and the father of lies."
>
> (John 8:42–44)

Jesus tells these people, who still think of themselves as his disciples, that their father is neither Abraham nor God, as they avow, but the devil. The reason for this judgment? These people have the devil for a father because it is the desires of the devil that they want to fulfill and not the desires of God. They take the devil as the *model* for their desires.

The desire of which Jesus speaks is therefore based on imitation, whether of the devil or of God. What our text is talking about is mimetic desire in the sense already defined. To repeat, the idea of "father" is here the same thing as the *model* without which human desire, lacking its own proper object, cannot come into being.

God and Satan are the two supreme models, "arch models," whose opposition to one another corresponds to what I have already described: one between models who never become obstacles and rivals for their disciples because they desire nothing in a greedy and competitive way and models whose greed for whatever they desire has immediate repercussions on their imitators, transforming them right away into diabolic obstacles. The first verses of our text are therefore an explicitly mimetic definition of desire and of the options for the human race that stem from it.

see 14

If the models that humans choose do not orient them in the right direction, one without conflict through Christ as intermediary, they expose themselves eventually to violent loss of differences and identity and thus to the single victim mechanism. And it is just here that we find the devil in the text of John. The sons of the devil are those who let themselves be taken into the circle of rivalistic desire and who, unknowingly, become the playthings of mimetic violence. Like all the victims of this process, "they don't know what they are doing" (Luke 23:34).

If we do not imitate Jesus, our models become the living obstacles that we also become for them. We descend together on the infernal spiral that leads to generalized mimetic crises and, ultimately, to the mimetic state of all against one. This inevitable consequence explains the apparently inexplicable shift of theme, the sudden allusion to collective murder:

Dante?

> From the beginning [the devil] was a murderer.

If readers do not find the mimetic cycle here, again it is because they do not understand it. They have the impression of an arbitrary, in-

explicable rupture between this sentence and those that precede it.
In reality the succession of themes is perfectly logical, corresponding
to the stages of the mimetic cycle. John attributes the mimetic all-
against-one to the devil because he already views him as the source
of the desire responsible for scandals. He could just as well attribute
the whole process to humans, and occasionally he does so.

The text from John is a new definition, ultrarapid but complete, of the mimetic cycle. In us and about us scandals proliferate;
sooner or later they carry us along toward mimetic snowballing and
the single victim mechanism. It makes us unknowingly the accomplices of <u>unanimous murders,</u> all the more deceived by the devil
because we are not aware of our own complicity, which is not
conscious of itself. We continue to imagine ourselves alien to all
violence.

From time to time people go all the way in accomplishing the
desires of their satanic father and fall back into the single victim mechanism. At the moment when Jesus speaks the word on
which we are commenting, the mechanism that formerly mobilized *But in*
the <u>Cainites</u> against Abel and subsequently thousands of crowds *Gen. it*
against thousands of single victims is at the point of being repeated *is Cain alone.*
against him.

Immediately after these fundamental assertions our text states
that the devil "has nothing to do with the truth." What makes him
our prince, or our "father," is <u>false accusation</u>, unjust <u>condemnation</u>
of an innocent victim. It is not based on anything real or objective,
but it succeeds no less in making itself unanimously convincing by
virtue of violent contagion. The primary meaning of Satan in the
Bible, we may recall, is the meaning found in the book of Job: the
chief prosecuting magistrate, the prosecutor in a case at court.

The devil is obviously untruthful, for if the persecutors understood the truth, the innocence of their victim, they could no longer
get rid of their own violence at this victim's expense. The single victim mechanism only functions by means of the ignorance of those
who keep it working. They believe they are supporting the truth
when they are really living a lie.

The devil's "quintessential being," the source from which he draws his lies, is the violent contagion that has no substance to it. The devil does not have a stable foundation; he has no *being at all*. To clothe himself in the semblance of being, he must act as a parasite on God's creatures. He is totally mimetic, which amounts to saying *nonexistent as an individual self.* The devil is also the father of lies; in certain manuscripts he is the father of "liars" because his deceitful violence has repercussions for generation after generation in human cultures. These cultures remain dependent on their founding murders and the rituals that reproduce them.

The Gospel of John scandalizes those who do not detect in it the choice it implies. The people to whom Jesus was speaking did not detect it either. Many people believe they are faithful to Jesus, and yet they address superficial reproaches to the Gospels. This shows that they remain subject to mimetic rivalries and their violent one-upmanship. If we don't see that the choice is inevitable between the two supreme models, God and the devil, then we have already chosen the devil and his mimetic violence.

Our righteous indignation against John's Gospel has no basis. Jesus speaks the truth to his questioners: they have chosen rivalistic desire, and the long-term consequences will be disastrous. The fact that these people are Jews is much less important than those exegetes who are a little too eager to convict the Gospels of anti-Semitism.

After its mimetic definition of desire, the Gospel of John makes the consequences of this desire explicit—satanic murder. The impression that Christian animosity toward the Jews produced this text is due to our misunderstanding of its content, so we imagine a series of gratuitous insults. This effect of our ignorance is often compounded by a preconceived hostility toward the gospel message.[3] We project our own resentment upon Christianity. John is talking to all

---

3. See 1 John 3:10, which speaks of "children of God and children of the devil" as a way of distinguishing those who love God and obey him and those who are lawless and sinners. The distinction has nothing to do with Christians vs. Jews. The author of 1 John was either the author of the Gospel or someone in the Johannine community.

humankind, not just to the Jews Jesus immediately addressed. This is usually the case in all the Gospels.

THE DEVIL, OR SATAN, signifies rivalistic contagion, up to and including the single victim mechanism. He may be located either in the entire process or in one of its stages. Modern exegetes, not recognizing the mimetic cycle, have the impression that since the word "Satan" means so many different things, it no longer means anything. This impression is deceptive. If we take up one by one the propositions I have analyzed, we easily see that this teaching is coherent. Far from being too absurd to deserve our attention, this Gospel theme contains incomparable knowledge of human conflict and the societies that are generated by the violent resolution of such conflict. Everything I have said about Satan corresponds to what the prior analysis of scandals enables us to understand. When the trouble caused by Satan becomes too great, Satan himself becomes his own antidote of sorts: he stirs up the mimetic snowballing and then the unanimous violence that makes everything peaceful once again.

The great parable of the murderous vine-growers (Matt. 21:33–41) brings out clearly the mimetic, or satanic, cycle. Each time the owner sends a messenger to the vine-growers, this message sets in motion a crisis among them, which they resolve by ganging up against the messenger and expelling him. This unanimous agreement is the height of the mimetic snowballing. Each violent expulsion is the completion of a mimetic cycle. The last messenger is the Son, expelled just like all the preceding messengers and finally murdered.

This parable confirms my definition of the Crucifixion. Jesus' death is one example among many others of the single victim mechanism. What makes the mimetic cycle of Jesus' suffering unique is, not the violence, but the fact that the victim is the Son of God, which is certainly the main thing from the standpoint of our redemption. However, if we neglect the anthropological substructure of the Passion, we will miss the true theology of the Incarnation, which makes little sense without this anthropological basis. The concepts of the mimetic cycle and the single victim mechanism give specific content to an idea of Simone Weil. She held that even before presenting a "theory of God," a *theology*, the Gospels offer a "theory of man," an *anthropology*.

Since it takes complete chaos in the community to set off the single victim mechanism, the Satan who expels and reestablishes order is really identical to the Satan who foments the disorder. Jesus' statement "Satan expels Satan" is irreplaceable.

What is the cure-all of the prince of this world, his most clever trick, perhaps his only resource? It is the mimetic all-against-one or single victim mechanism. It is the mimetic unanimity that, at the highest pitch of disorder, brings order back into human communities. This sleight of hand remained hidden until the Jewish and Christian revelation. In fact, it has, to an extent, remained hidden after the Christian revelation up to our own time since it remains almost universally misunderstood. Thanks to this deception, human communities are indebted to Satan for the shaky relative order that they enjoy. They are thus always in his debt and cannot free themselves on their own.

Satan imitates the same model as Jesus, God himself, but in a spirit of arrogance and rivalry for power. Satan has succeeded in perpetuating his own satanic kingdom for the better part of human history, thanks to God's forbearance. However, the mission of Jesus among human beings marks the beginning of the end for the prince of this world. The kingdom of Satan corresponds to that part of human history that precedes the death and resurrection of Christ, almost entirely governed by the single victim mechanism and the false religions it produces.

The mimetic concept of Satan enables the New Testament to give evil its due without granting it any reality or ontological substance in its own right that would make of Satan a kind of god of evil. Satan does not "create" by his own means. Rather he sustains himself as a parasite on what God creates by imitating God in a manner that is jealous, grotesque, perverse, and as contrary as possible to

the upright and obedient imitation of Jesus. To repeat, Satan is
an imitator in the rivalistic sense of the word. His kingdom is a
caricature of the kingdom of God. Satan is the ape of God.

To affirm that Satan has no actual being, as Christian theology
has done, means that Christianity does not oblige us to see him
as someone who really exists. The interpretation that assimilates
Satan to rivalistic contagion and its consequences enables us for
the first time to acknowledge the importance of the prince of this
world without also endowing him with personal *being*. Traditional
theology has rightly refused to do the latter.

In the Gospels, we found, mimetic and victimary phenomena
are organized around two different concepts. The first is an impersonal principle, scandal. The second is this mysterious figure that
the Gospels call "Satan" or "the devil." As we have seen, the synoptic Gospels contain a discourse of Jesus on scandal but no discourse
on Satan. The Gospel of John, on the other hand, includes no discourse on scandal, but it includes one on the devil, which we have
just examined.

Scandals and Satan are fundamentally the same thing. However,
we can observe two important differences between them. The primary emphasis in the two concepts shifts significantly. The accent
in scandal is on the early stages of the mimetic process, consequently on relations between individuals rather than on collective
phenomena—although the latter are not absent, as already noted.
The mimetic cycle is foreshadowed, but it does not take such clear
form as in the case of the figure of Satan, or the devil. The single
victim mechanism is suggested but not clearly set forth.

With scandals as our single starting point it would be difficult,
I think, to arrive at a complete explanation of the single victim
mechanism and the anthropological meaning of the Cross. Yet this
is what Paul does when he defines the Cross as the supreme scandal.
If we could not turn to the pattern of the mimetic cycle to interpret
it, Paul's message would remain partially unintelligible. Most readers
do not really understand what Paul means.

But with the satanic expulsion of Satan the mimetic cycle is really closed—the knot is really tied—for the single mechanism becomes explicitly defined.

But why doesn't Satan present himself as an impersonal principle in the same way as the scandals? Because he designates the principal consequence of the single victim mechanism, the emergence of a false transcendence and the numerous deities that represent it, Satan is always *someone*. This is what the following chapters should enable us to understand better.

Part Two

The Enigma of Myth
Resolved

Chapter 4

The Horrible Miracle
of Apollonius of Tyana

APOLLONIUS OF TYANA was a celebrated guru of the second century after Christ. Among the pagans his miracles were viewed as superior to those of Jesus. The most spectacular is certainly his healing of a plague epidemic in the city of Ephesus. We possess an account of it thanks to Philostratus, a Greek writer of the following century and the author of the *Life of Apollonius of Tyana*.

The Ephesians could not get rid of this epidemic. After many remedies that did not work, they turned to Apollonius who, by supernatural means, came to them in the blink of an eye and announced their immediate healing:

> "Take courage, for I will today put a stop to the course of
> the disease." And with these words he led the population en-
> tire to the theatre, where the image of the Averting god has
> been set up. [The Averting god in this case is Hercules, as will
> become clear later.] And there he saw what seemed an old
> mendicant artfully blinking his eyes as if blind, and he carried
> a wallet and a crust of bread in it; and he was clad in rags and
> was very squalid of countenance. Apollonius therefore ranged
> the Epheseians around him and said: "Pick up as many stones
> as you can and hurl them at this enemy of the gods." Now
> the Ephesians wondered what he meant, and were shocked at
> the idea of murdering a stranger so manifestly miserable; for
> he was begging and praying them to take mercy upon him.
> Nevertheless Apollonius insisted and egged on the Ephesians
> to launch themselves on him and not let him go. And as soon

49

as some of them began to take shots and hit him with their stones, the beggar who had seemed to blink and be blind, gave them all a sudden glance and showed that his eyes were full of fire. Then the Ephesians recognized that he was a demon, and they stoned him so thoroughly that their stones were heaped into a great cairn around him. After a little pause Apollonius bade them remove the stones and acquaint themselves with the wild animal which they had slain. When therefore they had exposed the object which they thought they had thrown their missiles at, they found that he had disappeared and in- stead of him there was a hound who resembled in form and look a Molosian dog, but was in size the equal of the largest lion; there he lay before their eyes, pounded to a pulp by their stones and vomiting foam as mad dogs do. Accordingly the statue of the Averting god, namely Hercules, has been set up over the spot where the ghost was slain.[1]

A more horrible miracle would be hard to find! If the author were Christian, he certainly would have been accused of slandering pa- ganism. But Philostratus is a militant pagan, resolved to defend the religion of his ancestors. He obviously viewed the murder of the beggar as able to lift up the morale of his coreligionists, to reinforce their resistance to Christianity. From the standpoint of public opin- ion, his calculation was sound. His book was so successful that Julian the Apostate put it back into circulation in the fourth century, as he made his last attempt to save paganism.

HOWEVER FANTASTIC the conclusion may be, Philostratus's narrative is too rich in concrete details to be completely invented. The miracle consists of triggering a mimetic contagion so powerful that it finally polarizes the entire population of the city against the unfortunate beggar. The initial refusal of the Ephesians is the sole ray of light in

---

1. Flavius Philostratus, *The Life of Apollonius of Tyana, the Epistles of Apollonius and the Treatise of Eusebius*, trans. F. C. Conybeare, Loeb Classical Library, 2 vols. (Cambridge, Mass.: Harvard University Press, 1912), 1:363–67.

this dark text, but Apollonius does everything he can to extinguish it, and he succeeds in doing so. The Ephesians start stoning their victim with such rage that they finally see him as Apollonius demands, the source of all their misfortunes, the "plague demon" that must be expelled in order to heal the city.

To describe the behavior of the Ephesians once the stoning begins, I am tempted to resort to a modern phrase: *letting off steam.* The more the Ephesians obey their guru, the more they are transformed into a violent mob and the more they let off steam, releasing their rage against the unfortunate beggar.

Another classic phrase comes to mind: the metaphor of the *abscess of fixation*[2] was often employed in the grand era of comparative religious studies. Apollonius channeled the violent contagion he released among the Ephesians toward a universally acceptable target, and thus he satisfies their appetite for violence, which takes a bit of time to awaken and which awakens only to be satisfied by the stoning of the victim designated by the guru. When their rage has been released, when the abscess of fixation has played its role, the Ephesians discover they are cured of their epidemic.

A third metaphor, not modern but ancient, is *catharsis,* or purification. Aristotle employs this word to describe the effect of the tragedies on the spectators. It means first of all the effect of sacrificial rituals, of bloody sacrifices, on those participating in them.

Apollonius's miracle embodies the kernel of a teaching rightly termed *religious,* which would escape us if we took the miracle to be imaginary. By no means an unheard-of phenomenon, alien to what we know about the Greek world, the stoning of the beggar recalls certain religious facts that are specifically Greek, the sacrifices of people called *pharmakoi.*[3] These sacrifices were real collective assas-

---

2. "Abscess of fixation" is a term that emerged in medical practice. An abscess is a wound festering with bacteria; an "abscess of fixation" is created artificially in order to purge the body of its impurities.

3. The Greek *pharmakoi,* singular *pharmakos,* refers to victims who were ritually beaten, driven out of cities, and killed, for example, by being forced over the edge of a precipice. The word *pharmakos,* designating a person who is selected as a ritual victim, is related to *pharmakon,* which means both "remedy" and "poison," depending on the context. In the story of the horrible miracle of Apollonius, the beggar is a *pharmakos,* a kind of ritual victim. Apollonius points to him as the

sinations of individuals similar to the beggar of Ephesus. I will return to this shortly.

The prestige of Apollonius is all the more sinister in that it may well have some basis in reality. The stoning passes for miraculous because it put an end to the complaints of the Ephesians. But you will say to me, "How could the murder of a beggar, no matter how unanimously committed, make a plague epidemic go away?"

In the ancient and medieval world the word "plague" was often used in a sense that is not strictly medical. Almost always it included a social dimension. Until the Renaissance, wherever "real" epidemics occurred, they disrupted social relations. Wherever social relations were disrupted, epidemics could occur. The fact that both kinds of plague are contagious facilitates the confusion.

If Apollonius had intervened in the context of a bacterial plague, the stoning would not have had any effect on the "epidemic." The clever guru must have gauged the situation and known that the city was prey to internal tensions that could be discharged on what we now call a *scapegoat*. This fourth metaphor designates a substitute victim, some innocent substitute for the real antagonists. In the *Life of Apollonius of Tyana*, just prior to the miracle itself, there is a passage that confirms our conjecture.

JUST BEFORE THE NARRATIVE of the miraculous stoning, Apollonius is in a seaport with some followers. There the sight of a ship about to depart inspires him to make some remarkable observations on order and disorder in societies. Apollonius sees the crew as a community whose success or failure depends on the nature of the relations between its members:

> Now if a single member of this community abandoned any one of his particular tasks or went about his naval duties in an inexperienced manner, they would have a bad voyage and would themselves impersonate the storm; but if they vie with

---

demon causing the plague (he is the source of pollution or poison), but his lynching restores the well being of Ephesus (he becomes the remedy for the crisis). — Trans.

one another and are rivals only with the object of one showing himself as good a man as the other, then their ship will make the best of all havens, and all their voyage will be one of fair weather and fair sailing, and the precaution they exercise about themselves will prove to be as valuable as if Poseidon our lord of safety, were watching over them.[4]

In short, there are good rivalries, and there are bad ones. There is the healthy emulation of those who "rival one another only in efficiency, each one doing his duty." There are the unhealthy rivalries of those who "do not master themselves." Not contributing at all to the smooth operation of societies, these unrestrained rivalries only weaken them. Those given over to them "will impersonate the storm." It's not external enemies that ruin societies; it's the unlimited ambitions, the unbridled competitions, that divide human beings rather than unite them. Philostratus does not define mimetic conflicts as extensively and powerfully as Jesus in his discourse on scandals, but he evidently speaks of the same type of conflict, and he speaks about it with unquestionable competence.

I have already suggested that the plague of Ephesus is not necessarily bacterial. It is an epidemic of mimetic rivalries, an interweaving of scandals, a war of *all against all*, which, thanks to the victim selected by the diabolical cleverness of Apollonius, is transformed "miraculously" into a reconciliation of *all against one*. Guessing the illness the Ephesians are suffering, the guru arouses violence against a miserable beggar. He expects from this violence a *cathartic* effect superior to that of ordinary sacrifices or of the tragic dramas that were performed, no doubt, in the theater of Ephesus in the second century of our era.

In my view, the warning against mimetic rivalries must be read as an introduction to the miracle. The passage I just cited immediately precedes the chapter devoted to the miraculous stoning, which I quoted in its entirety at the beginning of this chapter. This proximity cannot fail to be intentional.

---

4. Flavius Philostratus, *The Life of Apollonius of Tyana*, chap. 9, 300.

The stoning is an expression of *the single victim mechanism*, just like the Passion. It is even more effective than the Passion in its violent outcome since it is completely unanimous and the community feels it is completely cured of its "plague epidemic."

EUSEBIUS OF CAESAREA was aware of the harm that the *Life of Apollonius* did to Christianity. Eusebius, the first great historian of the Church, friend and collaborator of Constantine, composed a critique of this book, but modern readers will not find there what they are expecting. Eusebius sets out to show particularly that the miracles of Apollonius are not impressive at all. He never denounces the monstrous stoning, as we would expect of him. He reduces the debate, just like the partisans of the guru, to a mimetic rivalry between miracle workers. This helps us understand why Jesus always refused to emphasize his own miracles.

Never does Eusebius really define what decisively separates Apollonius and Jesus. When confronted with victims being stoned, Jesus is poles apart from Apollonius. Jesus doesn't instigate stonings; rather he does all he can to prevent them. Never does Eusebius really say what strikes the eyes of the modern reader. To take the measure of the two spiritual masters on this point, we must compare the "miracle" manipulated by Apollonius with a text that has nothing of the miraculous, that of the woman whose stoning Jesus prevents:

The scribes and the Pharisees brought before him a woman taken in adultery. Placing her in view of everyone, they said to Jesus, "Master, this woman was surprised in the act of adultery. Moses commanded us in the Law to stone such women. Now what do you say about it?" They said this to set a trap for him, in order to be able to accuse him. But Jesus, bending down, started writing with his finger on the ground. As they were insistent, he drew up and said to them: "Let whoever is without sin among you cast the first stone at her!" And, bending down again, he once more began to write on the ground. When he said this, they withdrew one by one, beginning with the oldest. Jesus remained, alone with the woman, who was still there. Then, standing up again, he said to her, "Woman, where are they? Has no one condemned you?" "No one, Lord," she answered. "Neither do I condemn you," Jesus said. "Go and sin no more." (John 8:3–11)

Contrary to the Ephesians, who are in a peaceful mood initially and opposed to stoning the beggar, the crowd that brings the adulterous woman to Jesus is in a combative mood. All the action in the two texts pivots on a problem that the single sentence of Jesus makes explicit, whereas it is never clarified by Philostratus: the problem of the first stone.

In the "miracle" of Apollonius the first stone is plainly the principal worry of the guru, since no Ephesian has the resolve to cast it. This worry is easy to detect, although it never becomes explicit. Apollonius finally resolves the difficulty in the way he desires, but he has to take great pains and work insidiously like the very devil he is. Jesus also overcomes the difficulties confronting him, but contrary to the guru, he exerts his influence against violence.

Jesus explicitly mentions the first stone. In fact, he emphasizes it as much as he can since he places it at the very end of his one-sentence intervention, prolonging its echo as long as possible, one might say, in the memory of his hearers: "Whoever is without sin among you, let him cast at her the first stone." The modern reader, skeptical, suspects a purely rhetorical effect: the first stone is proverbial. Cast the stone, cast the first stone: this is one of those expressions that everyone repeats.

Is this really just an "effect of language"? Let us remember that it is this very story of the woman taken in adultery and saved from stoning that has made "casting the first stone" proverbial. If this saying is still repeated everywhere today, in all the languages where Christianity has spread, it is because of our Gospel text, and it is repeated also because of its extraordinary relevance, underscored precisely by the parallelism of the two accounts.

When Apollonius orders the Ephesians to gather stones and throw them at the beggar, these good people refused to do it, and Philostratus naively discloses to us not only this refusal but the arguments justifying it. The Ephesians could not resolve, coldheartedly, to massacre a fellow human, miserable, disgusting, and insignificant though he was. The arguments justifying this refusal have their counterpart in the saying of Jesus. In this instance they are the equivalent, not of the very last words quoted, but the very first: "Whoever among you is without sin..." The Ephesians don't accept that they have the right coldly to assassinate a fellow creature in whom they have nothing to reproach.

To accomplish his ends, Apollonius has to distract the Ephesians from the deed he asks them to commit, so he tries to make them forget the physical reality of the stoning. With a ridiculous grandiloquence he denounces the beggar as an "enemy of the gods." To make the violence possible, he must demonize the individual he has selected as victim. And finally the guru succeeds. He obtains what he desires: the first stone. Once it is thrown, Apollonius can take a nap or whatever, for now violence and deceit are bound to triumph. The same Ephesians who had pity on the beggar a moment earlier now demonstrate a violent emulation of one another that is so relentless, so contrary to their initial attitude, that our surprise can only equal our sadness. Not purely rhetorical, the first stone is decisive because it is the most difficult to throw. Why is it the most difficult to throw? Because it is the only one without a *model*.

When Jesus finally responds, the first stone is the last obstacle that prevents the stoning. In calling attention to it, in mentioning it expressly, Jesus does all he can to reinforce this obstacle and magnify it. The more those thinking about throwing the first stone perceive the responsibility they would assume in throwing it, the greater the chance that they will let their hands fall and drop the stone.

Do we really need a mimetic model for an act as simple as throwing stones? Yes, when the target is a human being, most people do. The positive proof is the initial resistance of the Ephesians. It is certainly not in order to undermine the prestige of Apollonius that Philostratus tells us about his difficulties. These must be real.

Once the first stone is thrown, thanks to the encouragement of Apollonius, the second comes fairly fast, thanks to the example of the first; the third comes more quickly still because it has two models rather than one, and so on. As the models multiply, the rhythm of the stoning accelerates.

Saving the adulterous woman from being stoned, as Jesus does, means that he prevents the violent contagion from getting started. Another contagion in the reverse direction is set off, however, a contagion of nonviolence. From the moment the first individual gives up stoning the adulterous woman, he becomes a model who is imitated more and more until finally all the group, guided by Jesus, abandons its plan to stone the woman.

Our two texts are as opposed to one another as possible in spirit, and yet they resemble each other since they are two examples of mimetic escalation. Their independent origin makes this resemblance very significant. The texts help us better understand the dynamic of crowds that must be defined, not primarily by violence or by nonviolence, but by imitation, by contagious imitation.

The fact that Jesus' saying continues to play a metaphorical role universally understood in a world where ritual stoning no longer exists suggests that mimetic contagion remains as powerful today as in the past, though in forms now usually less violent. The symbolism of the first stone is still understandable because the mimetic definition of collective behavior remains just as valid now as it was two thousand years ago, even if the physical act of stoning is no longer practiced. In order to suggest the tremendous role of violent contagion in human culture, Jesus does not resort to the abstract terms that we can hardly do without: imitation, contagion, mimesis, etc. The first stone suffices. This unique saying permits him to point to the true principle not only of ancient stonings but of all crowd phenomena, ancient and modern.[5]

---

5. See my interpretation of this same passage from John in *Quand ces choses commenceront*

Apollonius must induce one or the other of the Ephesians—it doesn't matter which one—to throw the first stone. But he doesn't want to call too much attention to it, and this is why he says nothing expressly about the first stone. Apollonius thus shows his duplicity. He is silent for reasons that match yet oppose Jesus' motive when he explicitly mentions the first stone and gives it as much emphasis as possible.

The Ephesians' initial hesitation and final relentlessness are so characteristic of violent contagion that our two accounts must portray realistically, accurately the dynamic structure, which is to say the "mimetic structure," of stoning a victim. In order to trigger unanimous violence the instigator must hide its mimetic nature, and this is what Apollonius does. But to discourage this same violence, light must be shed upon that same nature. The truth about it must be expressed. This is what Jesus does when he emphasizes "the first stone."

THIS SAYING OF JESUS, like many memorable sayings, is not original and novel in the way that the modern world appreciates when it demands of its writers and artists an originality in the sense of what has never been said or heard—novelty at all costs. The response of Jesus to the challenge thrown up to him is not original in that sense. Jesus does not invent the idea of the first stone, but he draws it from the Bible; he is inspired by his religious tradition.

Legal stoning does not coincide with the arbitrary assassination plotted by Apollonius. The Law of Moses provides for stoning in the case of well-defined offenses. Moreover, because the Law fears false denunciations, to make these more difficult it requires the informants, a minimum of two, to cast the first two stones themselves.

Jesus transcends the Law, but in the Law's own sense and direction. He does this by appealing to the most humane aspect of the legal prescription, the aspect most foreign to the contagion of vio-

---

(Paris: Arléa, 1994), 179–86. See also R. Girard, *La Vittima e la folla*, trans. and ed. Giuseppe Fornari (Treviso: Santi Quaranta, 1998), 95–132.

lence, which is the obligation of the two accusers to throw the first two stones. The Law deprives the accusers of a mimetic model.

Once the first stones are thrown, all the community must join in the stoning. To maintain order in ancient societies, there was sometimes no other means than this mechanism of contagion and mimetic unanimity. The Law resorts to this without hesitation, but as prudently, as parsimoniously as possible. Jesus intends to go beyond the provisions for violence in the Law, being in agreement on this point with many fellow Jews of his time. However, he acts always in the direction and spirit of the biblical revelation and not against it.

THE EPISODE of the adulterous woman is one of the rare successes Jesus had in his dealings with a crowd. This success brings out by contrast his many failures and especially, of course, the role of the crowd in his own death.

In the Gospel episode of the woman taken in the act of adultery, if Jesus had not convinced the crowd, if the stoning had taken place, Jesus would have risked being stoned himself. Failing to save a victim threatened with collective lynching, being the only person at her side in face of the crowd, is to run the risk of suffering her fate also. This principle is found in all ancient societies. In the period preceding the Crucifixion Jesus himself, the Gospels tell us, narrowly escaped various attempts to stone him. Jesus does not always get off so easily, and he finally played the same role as the beggar of Ephesus by suffering the torture reserved for the lowest of the low in the Roman Empire. Between him and the beggar there is a resemblance in death and also a resemblance before death, a resemblance in their behavior as each faced the threatening crowd.

Before responding to those who ask his advice about the obligation to stone adulterous women that is written in the Law of Moses, Jesus bends over toward the ground and writes in the dust with his finger. It is not with the intention of writing, in my opinion, that Jesus bends over. It is rather because he is bent that he writes. He bends over to avoid the gaze of these men with bloodshot eyes.

If Jesus returned their looks, these angry men would not see his look as it really is but would transform it into a mirror of their own anger. Their own challenge, their own provocation, is what they would read in the look of Jesus, no matter how peaceable it really is, and they would feel provoked in return. The confrontation could no longer be avoided and would bring about what Jesus is trying to prevent, the stoning of the victim. Jesus avoids thus even the shadow of provocation.

When Apollonius orders the Ephesians to arm themselves with stones and gather in a circle around the beggar, the latter reacts in a way reminiscent of the behavior of Jesus facing the angry crowd. He too does not want to give these threatening men the impression that he is defying them. His desire to pass for blind, even if it is exclusively "professional" at the outset, corresponds, in my view, to the gesture of Jesus' writing in the dust. The beggar does not want to look back at his potential assailants. When the stones begin to rain down, he can no longer hope to get away by pretending not to see what is happening about him. His maneuver has failed. So he no longer hesitates to look all around, hoping against hope to discover a breach in the wall of his attackers that would allow him to flee. In the look of the beast tracked down and trapped that the beggar gives the Ephesians, they perceive a kind of defiance. Only at this moment do they believe they recognize their victim as the demon invented by Apollonius. The scene confirms and justifies the caution of Jesus:

> And as soon as some of them began to take shots and hit him with their stones, the beggar who had seemed to blink and be blind, gave them all a sudden glance and showed that his eyes were full of fire. Then the Ephesians recognized that he was a demon. . . .

The stoning of the beggar makes us think of the Crucifixion. Jesus is finally swept away by a mimetic escalation like the stoning of the beggar. The escalation that he succeeds in reversing in the case of the adulterous woman, in his own case he is unable to prevent. This is just what the crowd gathered at the foot of the Cross understands after its own fashion: mocking the powerlessness of Jesus to do for himself what he has done for others, they cry out, "He who saved others cannot save himself!"

The Cross is the equivalent of the Ephesus stoning. To say that Jesus identifies himself with all victims is to say that he identifies himself not only with the adulterous woman or the Suffering Servant but also with the beggar of Ephesus. Jesus *is* this poor wretch of a beggar.

Chapter 5

Mythology

THE MIRACLE OF APOLLONIUS involves converting an epidemic of mimetic rivalries into a state of unanimous violence whose "cathartic" effect restores tranquility and strengthens social ties among the Ephesians. The entire city sees the stoning as a supernatural sign. To confirm this miraculous interpretation and make it official, they announce that Heracles has intervened. He is the right god for the role because he is already on the spot, represented by his statue in the theater where the stoning takes place. Rather than condemn the criminal attack on the beggar, the municipal authorities ratify the miracle, and Apollonius becomes quite a celebrity.

The god played no role in the event, so this linkage to official paganism may appear artificial to us. The appeal to religion, however, is not arbitrary in principle. Between the stoning instigated by Apollonius and the ancient forms and features of the sacred, the affinities are real.

Many myths have important features similar to the miracle of Apollonius, but the violence, even when the lynching can be detected, is not generally described with the realism of a Philostratus. If we look at literary texts, Ovid's *Metamorphoses*, for example, the proliferation of fantastic elements veil the horror of a spectacle that is never really *represented* to the reader the way it is in Philostratus's account.

The myths almost always begin with a state of extreme disorder. This chaos is not usually presented as "original." Often it is possible to detect behind it a breakdown or failure of some sort, whether in the community, in nature, or in the cosmos.

What disturbs the peace frequently is an "epidemic" that is ill defined, similar to the one in the stoning at Ephesus. It may also be quite explicitly a social malaise, a conflict whose mimetic character is suggested by the important mythic role of *twins* or *enemy brothers*. The conflict may also unfold between innumerable other beings, mythic or legendary: monsters, stars, mountains, or whatever, but these beings enter into conflict and battle each other as mimetic doubles. In place of disorder in the beginning of the myths there /
may be an interruption of vital functions, a kind of paralysis. Claude ㄹ
Lévi-Strauss has scrutinized this aspect of mythic beginnings, but he failed to detect a connection with violence. It may be a matter also of more ordinary disasters: famines, floods, destructive droughts, and ₃
other natural catastrophes. In all cases the initial mythic situation can be summarized in terms of a crisis that threatens the community and its cultural system with total destruction.

The crisis is usually resolved by violence, which is either collective or gives off echoes of collective action. The only great exception is the *dual* violence stemming from the struggle between two brothers or enemy twins, and one of the two triumphs over the other. This sort of myth always alludes to an escalation of imitation, which is rivalistic and disintegrating *before* the violence but reconciliatory and unifying *after* the violence and because of it, which is not apparent except for the light shed in the preceding analysis of the miracle of Apollonius. The miracle of Apollonius itself is clarified by the Gospels and the concept of the mimetic cycle, which was spelled out in my first three chapters.

At the height of the crisis the unanimous violence is set off. In many myths that appear to be the oldest, and which I think actually are, the violent unanimity is presented as a sudden mass movement more suggested than really described; it is quite clear in rituals. The rituals visibly *reproduce* the unanimous, reconciling violence of the single victim mechanism.

The protagonist in the old myths is the entire community transformed into a violent mob. They believe that an isolated individual threatens them, a person who is often a foreigner, and they spontaneously massacre the visitor. This type of violence is found in classical Greece, in the sinister cult of Dionysos.

The attackers rush as one upon their victim. The collective hysteria is such that they literally behave like beasts of prey. They manage to dismember this victim, tear him apart with their hands, with their nails, with their teeth, as if anger or fear made their physical power ten times as great. Sometimes they consume the corpse. The French language does not have a proper term to designate this sudden, convulsive violence, this pure crowd phenomenon. The word that comes most readily to the lips is an Americanism, "lynching."

I cannot accept the interpretations that hold that the innumerable variants of this collective murder, or murder collectively inspired, refer to nothing real. Given all the evidence in mythology and biblical texts, given the realism of certain descriptions, given the real violence of the rituals, I think a purely "symbolic" interpretation, the invocation of some fantasy or another, to explain all these scenes of violence is dictated by a systematic prejudice against the real. I reject it without the least hesitation, if for no reason other than its inability to lead the study of mythology out of the impasse in which it has been trapped for so long.

Since lynching a victim with bare hands plays a significant role in ancient myths, why not try out the simplest hypothesis, the most logical one: behind the myths is real violence analogous in savage ferocity to the stoning at Ephesus? Mimetic conflicts are real, leading regularly to collective violence, so why not suppose that there is real violence behind most of the myths?

If the lynchers tear apart their victim with their own hands, they must be without weapons. If they had weapons, they would use them. If they don't have them, it's because they didn't think they needed them. They had come together for peaceful reasons, to welcome a visitor perhaps, and suddenly things went wrong....

THE EVENTS of collective violence of which I have spoken so far, the Ephesus stoning, the Passion, the decapitation of John the Baptist, are more or less manipulated. We can observe also, in myths, many spontaneous lynchings. These must reflect powerful mimetic snowballing phenomena, which were not restrained by legal and institutional obstacles. Somewhere anger flames up, a panic is set off, and all the community is thrown into violence by the working of instantaneous contagion.

In societies without a judicial system, contagious indignation explodes in the form of the lynch mob. Louis Gernet sees lynching as a primitive mode of justice,[1] which is better than seeing nothing at all, of course, but in my view the investigator here reverses the genesis of the process. He does not see that the point of departure in archaic religion, and finally in all the violence labeled judicial, is the violent unanimity of spontaneous lynching, which is unpremeditated. This spontaneous lynching is what reestablishes peace and, with the victim as intermediary, gives this peace a religious, a divine, meaning. Once the victim is killed the crisis is over, peace is regained, the plague is healed, all the elements become calm again, chaos withdraws, what is blocked or locked or paralyzed is opened, the incomplete is completed, gaps are filled, and the confusion of differences is restored to proper differentiation.

The transformation of the evildoer into a divine benefactor is a phenomenon simultaneously marvelous and routine. In most cases the myths don't even indicate this change. The one who is lynched at the beginning of the myth because he or she came as destroyer of the totemic system—lo and behold—presides in the end over the reconstruction of this same system or over the construction of a new one. Unanimous violence has transformed the evildoer into a divine benefactor in a manner so extraordinary, yet nevertheless ordinary, that most of the myths do not say anything about this metamorphosis.

All this is explicable if we see that by the end of these myths unanimous violence has reconciled the community and the reconciling power is attributed to the victim, who is already "guilty," already "responsible" for the crisis. The victim is thus transfigured

---

1. Louis Gernet, *Droit et institutions en Grèce antique* (Paris: Flammarion, 1982).

twice: the first time in a negative, evil fashion; the second time in a positive, beneficial fashion. Everyone thought this victim had perished, but it turns out he or she must be alive since this very one reconstructs the community immediately after destroying it. He or she is clearly immortal and thus divine. So the conclusion must be that the myths themselves reflect, though in a confused and altered fashion, the process that the Gospels enable us to see and that we found subsequently in the Ephesus stoning.

This process characterizes myths in general. The same human groups that expel and massacre individuals on whom suspicions fall switch over to adoring them when they find they are calm and reconciled. What reconciles them, to repeat, is nothing else than projecting on the victim all their fears in the beginning and subsequently all their hopes once they become reconciled. These are disorders characteristic of human groups that paradoxically, as they become more and more aggravated, afford humans the means of creating forms of organization. These new forms emerge from a crisis of violence and then put an end to it. Lynchings restore peace at the expense of the divinized victim. This is why they are associated with manifestations of this divine figure and the communities recall them in transfigured accounts that we call "myths."

IN THE MIRACULOUS STONING associated with Apollonius of Tyana no new deity appears. However, the event is not far removed from such an apparition since the beggar is perceived as a supernatural being, the plague demon. After the stoning the murderers don't recognize their victim. The bit of human appearance that old age and misery have not destroyed in the beggar, the stones have finished destroying. The unfortunate man is not stoned because he is monstrous; he becomes a monster because of the stoning. The Ephesians have thrown their stones with such fury that the corpse of the beggar appears "pounded to a pulp."

The author seems to hesitate at this point: the demon is as large as a lion and yet is not a lion but a dog. To make this description of the monster more respectable, Philostratus has him vomit foaming saliva "like rabid dogs," but this transformation is scarcely impressive or convincing; it is too transparent to conceal the sad truth. Here we have only a pale form of myth. The unanimous murder is not transformed sufficiently to be divinized. This is why a new deity does not appear. We know what this stoning lacks to produce a god: a sufficiently powerful event of collective violence. If the collective violence were more powerful, the beggar would be divinized.

The healing gods in mythology are manifested first of all in forms that resemble the miracle of Apollonius. The demons initially responsible for the illness are subsequently the ones who heal it. If these gods are considered capable of healing the illnesses that they transmit to humans, it is because the violence executed against them, when they appear as evil, contagious, and demonic, has a reconciling effect similar to that of our stoning, but more powerful. Here it is the efficacious "abscess of fixation" that is divinized.

The victims who arouse the most terror in the first phase arouse the most relief and harmony in the second. They are thus transformed twice, as I said, but this does not occur in the instance of the beggar of Ephesus.

In the Oedipus myth the role of the god Apollo is a good example of double transformation. This is the god believed to send the epidemic and to punish those who shelter an abominable criminal within their walls, a son who murders his father and has sex with his mother. At first Apollo comes across as no more than a plague demon. Once Oedipus is expelled, Thebes finds itself cured. Apollo has rewarded the obedience of the people of Thebes, and he puts an end to a blackmail that would be henceforth without reason. Since Apollo *is* the plague himself, he only has to go away to put an end to it.

In the miracle of Apollonius, Heracles is a figurehead held above the stoning of the beggar exactly as Apollo stands over the expulsion of the hero in the Oedipus myth. Apollo remains indispensable in this last example in spite of the fact that the hero, unlike the beggar, is somewhat divinized. However, he is not sufficiently divinized to confer on him the identity of a deity, and so the myth resorts to a great preexisting god, Apollo, as in the miracle story. If the transformational power were stronger in the miracle of Apollonius, the divinization of the beggar would follow his demonization. The second transformation would conceal the horror of the scene. We would then have a true myth rather than the incomplete, hybrid story reported by Philostratus.

Though the miracle of Apollonius is only a pale form of myth, it is this anemic, incomplete character that makes it so interesting for understanding the origins of myth. The account breaks into two separate phases a genesis that, in the myths properly so called, is presented in a form so compact that it appears undecipherable. Only the first transformation is present in Philostratus; it alone is visible in his account, and that is indeed why we are horrified. The second transformation is completely absent, and so Heracles is called to the rescue as a replacement in this absence.

The first sentence of the account contains the first reference to the god:

> [Apollonius] led the population entire to the theatre, where the image of the Averting god has been set up. . . .

The god is not mentioned as the story continues until the very end of the account:

> For this reason [the "miracle"] the statue of the Averting god, namely Hercules, has been set up over the spot where the ghost was slain.

The two mentions of Heracles frame the entire event and give it its religious meaning. When it's all said and done, the true author of the miracle is held to be the god: he decided to exercise his protective function through an inspired intermediary, Apollonius of Tyana.

The miraculous stoning is not a complete myth but half a myth. This half is the first part of mythic structure, which is the most hidden in a complete myth, and it is better not to know or suspect the existence of this part if we glorify myths the way many now do. To preserve their neo-pagan illusions, they must turn away from texts that are too revealing, such as the stoning instigated by Apollonius.

Philostratus describes the stoning in a manner so honestly realistic that he unintentionally sheds light on the process of which he himself, paradoxically, remains ignorant. There is no reason to think that he is particularly sadistic or that he is different from most of his coreligionists. He remains attached to his ancestral religion, but he doesn't see it as it is. He describes its obvious workings without really perceiving them himself. The horror his account inspires in us would no doubt deeply astonish him.

In Philostratus's religious imagination the great god Pan is not completely dead. It is not by accident that this god of violent mobs is the symbol of classic mythology. From his name comes our word "panic."[2] This god has not lost all his power of enchantment over the author of the *Life of Apollonius*.

WHY DO THE GOSPELS, in their most complete definition of the mimetic cycle, have recourse to a figure named Satan or the devil rather than to an impersonal principle? I think the principal reason is that the human subjects as individuals are not aware of the circular process in which they are trapped; the real manipulator of the process is *mimetic contagion itself*. There is no real subject within this mimetic contagion, and that is finally the meaning of the title "prince of this world," if it is recognized that Satan *is* the absence of being.

Satan is not at all divine, but in naming him we allude to something essential that I mentioned briefly in my chapter about him, a matter of great interest in this book: the origin of primitive and pagan gods. Even if Satan's transcendence is false, totally without reality in a religious sense, on the worldly plane his works are undeniable and formidable. Satan is the absent subject of structures of disorder and order, which stem from rivalistic relations among

---

2. "Pan" as the name of the god comes from the neuter form of the adjective meaning "all" or "every" in Greek. "Panic" among humans is the chaos and terror that results from everyone blindly imitating the desires of everyone else. — Trans.

humans. When it's all said and done, these rivalries both organize and disorganize human relations.

Satan is mimetic contagion as its most secret power, the creation of the false gods out of the midst of which Christianity emerged. To speak of the mimetic cycle in terms of Satan enables the Gospels to say or to suggest many things about the religions perceived by Christianity as false, deceptive, and illusory that they could not say in the language of scandal, the reconciling power of unanimous violence.

The peoples of the world do not invent their gods. They deify their victims. What prevents researchers from discovering this truth is their refusal to grasp the real violence behind the texts that represent it. The refusal of the real is the number one dogma of our time. It is the prolongation and perpetuation of the original mythic illusion.[3]

Jenny Events: RG himself does this w/ Satan (45)

---

3. On all the questions raised by this chapter, and for examples of myths "mimetically" interpreted, see Richard J. Golsan, *René Girard and Myth* (New York and London: Garland Publishing, 1993).

Chapter 6

Sacrifice

THANKS TO THE TALENT of Philostratus, the violence of the Ephesians, at first so moved by compassion for their victim, is displayed with a realism so modern that we cannot elude its representation. As enamored as we are of myth, we cannot fail to understand the role of violent unanimity in the illusion that mythology creates.

The primitive sacred is generated by mimetic snowballing and the single victim mechanism. The communities pacified and reconciled by their victims are too conscious of their inability to become reconciled by their own actions not to imagine that some god has brought them together, and that god has to be that same victim who inflicted evil on them but who now bestows benefits on them.

In the miracle of Apollonius the experience is not intense enough to bring about the second transformation, in which the victim who was demonized is turned into the god who bestows benefits. That is why the admirers of our guru found it necessary to resort to a god of the traditional pantheon in order to lend support to the miracle. If the experience of mimetic contagion had been stronger, the persecutors would have attributed their deliverance directly to their victim, who would take on the roles of both evil demon and beneficent deity.

When the transforming power weakens, the second transference, the divinization of the victim, disappears first. The first transference (scapegoat), not the second, is certainly present in our story. The more precarious of the two, the second transference, when it emerges, covers up the demonic and conceals from human eyes what

71

Philostratus obliges us to contemplate: the projection of the community's accumulated scandals on the unfortunate beggar, mimetic violence, the foundation of primitive religion in its totality.

Philostratus is not sensitive to violence in the way our historical era obliges us to be. Such lack of sensitivity, so shocking to us, is one of the historical problems that the analyses I offer should help us to grasp.

THE DOUBLE TRANSFERENCE of the primitive sacred explains the logical flaw that characterizes numerous myths. In the beginning of the latter the hero passes for a dangerous criminal and nothing more. After the violence intended to prevent him or her from inflicting further harm on the community, this same scapegoat appears in the conclusion as the divine savior, though this change of identity is never justified or even pointed out. At the end of these myths the criminals of the beginning, now duly divinized, preside at the reconstruction of the cultural system they seem to have destroyed in the initial phase when they were the object of hostile projections, when they were only scapegoats.

Formerly religion was regarded as "dreamlike," as "fantastic." Today it is celebrated as "playful creation." In reality, world mythology is very close to the type of fable creation that has always been generated by collective violence in all traditional societies, and even again somewhat in the medieval period when great *panics* occurred, occasioned by calamities such as the black plague. The victims then were Jews, lepers, foreigners, the disabled, the marginal people of every kind—the "excluded," we say in our time.

In the medieval instances the mythic transformation is still weaker than in Philostratus's text, and in our day the demystification I am proposing does not scandalize anyone at all, for it is perceived as so evident that it goes without saying. It is the opposite attitude that would scandalize our contemporaries, that is, if we did not recognize in these medieval phenomena the scapegoat violence that they truly embody. What we still refuse to see is that foundational myths embody the same violence as well.

WE CAN, starting from the preceding analyses, compare the origin of myths and their later, weaker versions to the action of a volcano now extinct. When it was active, this volcano produced "real" myths, but it spewed out so much lava and smoke that it was impossible to lean over the crater to see what was happening inside.

The stoning at Ephesus is the work of this same volcano in a later period. It is still glowing but has cooled off enough that one can approach it. Though not completely inactive, it produces only truncated myths, amputated, limited to hostile transference upon a victim. The beggar of Ephesus never becomes an object of adoration. The miraculous stoning produces only a mediocre little demon.

So I see the account given by Philostratus as a precious "missing link" between the full mythological transformations on the one hand, which are not directly decodable, and the transformations easy to decode on the other hand, such as the medieval witch-hunt. The kinship of the witch-hunt to mythology properly so called becomes evident in the light shed by Philostratus and the Gospels.

In both cases we have collective violence revolving around a false interpretation, governed as it is by the unanimous illusion of the persecutors. Standing before the myths, we remain the dupes of transformations that are no longer capable of fooling us in the case of the witch-hunt. When we deal with the persecutions that occur in our historical world, we can see through the lies of the persecutors and understand that the victims must be real and must be viewed as innocent even though the persecutions are far removed in time. We understand that we would be not only foolish but would incur guilt to deny the innocence of the victims. We don't want to make ourselves accomplices of the witch-hunt. Mythology is a more powerful version of the transformational process whose functioning we demystify easily in the witch-hunt because the process doesn't work any longer in our world, except in very weakened form, one incapable of producing true myths.

Myths properly named are part of the same textual family as the stoning instigated by Apollonius, the medieval phenomenon of the witch-hunt, or again . . . the Passion of Christ. Reports of collective violence are <u>intelligible in inverse proportion to the degree of</u> <u>transformation they have undergone.</u> The most transformed are the myths, and <u>the least transformed of all is the Passion of Christ,</u> the only account that completely reveals the cause of violent unanimity, which is mimetic contagion, the contagion of violence. What I am arguing, in short, is that the mythology that appears most noble, that of the Olympian gods, depends on the same textual origin as the demonization of the Ephesus beggar or the medieval witches.

The connection of mythology and the witch-hunt may seem scandalous because of the aesthetic and cultural veneration with which we surround mythology, but our sense of outrage must dissolve before a serious comparison of the two structures. In both instances we find the same facts organized in the same fashion, though they have become much weakened in our so-called "historical" world, our Christian world.

As the gods age, of course, their evil dimension becomes blurred to the advantage of their beneficent side, but vestiges of the original demon always remain, that is, of the victim who was collectively massacred. If we are content to repeat the standard clichés about the Olympian gods, we will see only their majesty and their serenity. In classical art the positive elements are generally in the foreground, but behind them, even in the case of Zeus, there are the "wild pranks" of the god, as they are called with an indulgence that is a little silly. Everyone agrees to "excuse" these escapades with a knowingly complicit smile, as if it were a little like youth who "sow their wild oats" or like an <u>American president</u> caught in a flagrant act of adultery. The escapades of Zeus and his fellow gods are supposedly only "weak shadows of their divine grandeur."

In reality the "wild pranks" are the traces of crimes similar to those of Oedipus and other divinized scapegoats: parricide, incest, bestial fornication, and other horrible crimes. All of these <u>are accusations</u> <u>typical of witch-hunts,</u> with which primitive mobs are permanently obsessed, as are modern crowds seeking to find victims. The "wild pranks" are essential to the primitive phenomenon of divinity.

Thank God for the historians of the Middle Ages! They refuse to deny the reality of witch-hunts. The phenomena they decode are too numerous, too intelligible, and too well documented to be easily sacrificed, so far at least, to the god of turning these matters into fiction that has taken hold of our philosophers and mythologists. The historians continue to affirm the actual existence of the victims massacred by medieval mobs: lepers, Jews, foreigners, women, those who are disabled, marginal persons of every sort. We would be not only naïve but guilty if we tried to deny the reality of these victims under the pretext that all such "stories" are obviously "imaginary," that in any case the "truth" as such does not exist, etc.

Now if the victims of the medieval witch-hunts are real, why wouldn't the victims of these myths also be? What prevents the mythologists from discovering the truth is, not the intrinsic difficulty of the task, but their excessive respect for ancient Greece, a respect that has lasted for centuries and that has come to be extended to all non-Western cultures. This undue respect is a function of the anti-Western and especially anti-Christian ideology that prevents the demystification of mythic forms, which we are now really in a position to decipher.

I am waiting with impatience for the day when scholars finally realize that in the myths they are dealing with the same themes as in the witch-hunts. Though these myths are structured in the same fashion, they are falsely perceived as indecipherable. The truth is, they have been deciphered for two thousand years. The Gospel Passion accounts have solved the riddle.

The interpretation I propose is not at all absurd or fantastic; rather it becomes evident from the moment we approach it from the angle of the "missing link" that we find in the stoning of the Ephesus beggar, which mediates between the reports of collective violence still capable of deceiving us, being mythic in the strong sense, and those in which we immediately recognize the illusions of persecutors mystified by their own acts of persecution.

THE STONING at Ephesus is of great interest because it demolishes the overly rigid distinctions of those who would prefer to imprison reality in well-defined categories. Linguistic structuralism avoids focusing upon texts like the one written by Philostratus, and for good reason. Philostratus steps over too many barriers that are now viewed as insuperable. Behind the discontinuity of language, our "missing link" makes visible a real continuity, bearing a real intelligibility, which cannot be locked up in the watertight compartments of ancient and modern classifiers. The famous linguistic methods are much appreciated nowadays because they replace the search for truth with structuralist word games.

The Ephesus stoning is not properly speaking a myth, and yet with the aid of the Gospels it has suggested to us a hypothesis about the nature and origin of myths and gods that comes as a direct extension of this text, a hypothesis difficult to reject for those who still believe in reality. The same holds for ritual sacrifices. While the Ephesus stoning is not strictly a sacrifice, it visibly maintains close ties to a certain type of sacrifice widespread in the Greek world. It is immediately reminiscent of a ritual that is so close to what Philostratus recounts that it is tempting to have recourse to it for a definition of the "miracle" of Apollonius: it is the ritual of the *pharmakos.*

The beggar picked by Apollonius recalls the kind of homeless persons whom Athens and the great Greek cities fed at their expense in order to make use of them as *pharmakoi* when the appointed time arrived, that is, collectively to assassinate them—why back away before the proper term?—during the Thargelia and other Dionysian festivals. Before stoning these poor wretches, the torturers sometimes struck or whipped their sexual organs and in general made them submit to a full round of ritual torture.

Apollonius knows what he is doing when he chooses a victim no one will mourn, for in this way he doesn't risk aggravating the disorder he is trying to pacify. It is good strategy. The beggar stoned displays all the classical features of the *pharmakos*, features we see likewise in all the human victims of sacrificial rituals. To avoid arousing reprisals, the torturers choose social nobodies: the homeless, those without family, the disabled and ill, abandoned old people, all those in short who bear the preferential signs for being selected as victims, the signs I discussed in *The Scapegoat*.[1] These signs or features change hardly at all from one culture to another. Their constancy contradicts cultural relativism. In our own day they still determine acts of "exclusion." Those who bear them are no longer murdered, and that is progress, though it is precarious and limited.

We hear it suggested, all too easily, that the Greeks of the classical era were "too civilized" to be devoted still to rituals as barbarous as that of the *pharmakos*. Some will argue, though without evidence to support it, that these rituals must have quickly fallen into disuse. But our miraculous stoning, some six centuries after Socrates and Plato, does not confirm this rosy optimism. ← *if it really happened*

The Dionysian cult carried on rites even more atrocious than the miracle of Apollonius, but we do not *see* them literally... not in *of violence in bk.* the sense in which the account by Philostratus, almost like a film, forces us to *see* the stoning at Ephesus. The blinking eyes of the *trag.* beggar, the crust of bread in his sack, the initial compassion of the *offstage.* Ephesians—all these concrete details increase the evocative power *reported.* of Philostratus's text. It would be tempting to conclude that even if the event narrated is real, it must be too exceptional to figure in a debate over violence in the pagan religions. To the contrary, I say, the account Philostratus gives us is not exceptional at all, except for its realism and its relative modernism.

The *pharmakos* rituals were supposed to purify the Greek cities of their illnesses and render them more harmonious; they were supposed, in short, to accomplish the kind of miracle that Apollonius worked with his beggar. In a period of crisis, all sacrificial cultures resort to rituals not provided in the normal liturgical calendar. The stoning of the beggar is an improvised *pharmakos* ritual. In having the beggar stoned, Apollonius inflicted on a human victim the unanimous violence that most sacrifices no longer reproduced in his period except on animal victims.

Theater performances are also rooted in collective violence and are a form of ritual, though even more cleansed of violence than

---

1. *The Scapegoat* (Baltimore: Johns Hopkins University Press, 1986), chap. 2: "Stereotypes of Persecution."

animal sacrifices. They are culturally richer than the animal sacrifices since they are, at least indirectly, meditations on the origins of
religion and culture as a whole. As such they are potential sources
of knowledge, as Sandor Goodhart shows us in his *Sacrificing Commentary.*[2] But the goal of tragedy is the same as sacrifice. It always
aims at producing among the members of the community a ritual
purification, the Aristotelian *catharsis*, which is an intellectualized
or "sublimated" version of the original sacrificial effect.

IN THE PERIOD when sacrificial rites were still effective in some cultures, when researchers asked people in the communities why they
practiced them so carefully, they always got the same double response. According to the peoples directly involved, and perhaps it
is time to listen to what they believed, sacrifices were intended (1) to
please the gods, who had prescribed them to the community, and
(2) to consolidate or restore, if need be, the order and peace of the
community. In spite of the unanimity of these responses, anthropologists have never taken them seriously. I think this is why they
have never resolved the enigma of sacrifice. To resolve it, we must
accept that the sacrificers were telling the truth as they understood
it. They were much closer to the explanation of their own rituals
than all our contemporary specialists.
    Bloody sacrifices are attempts to repress or moderate the internal
conflicts of primitive or archaic communities, and they do this by
reproducing as exactly as possible, at the expense of the victims
substituted for the original victim, a real act of violence that had
occurred in the indeterminate past. This original violence had really
reconciled these communities, thanks to its unanimity.
    The gods are always involved in the sacrifices because the collec-
tive acts of violence the sacrifices intend to reproduce are the same
ones that, at some point in the past, had spontaneously reconciled
these communities. And because the communities are reconciled, the
beneficiaries are persuaded that the victims are divine. In short, it is al-

2. Sandor Goodhart, *Sacrificing Commentary* (Baltimore: Johns Hopkins University Press, 1996).

ways an effective "single victim mechanism" that works as a model for
the sacrifices, because it has really ended a mimetic crisis, an epidemic
of multiple acts of vengeance that the community could not control.

The proof that sacrifices are modeled after real acts of violence is
that their fundamental structural features are always the same even
if they differ in details. It is obviously the model of spontaneous
collective violence that inspires them. The resemblances between
sacrificial systems from one end of the earth to the other are certainly too constant and explicable to lend credence to the imaginary
or psychological concepts of sacrifice.

To UNDERSTAND how these rituals are born, let us imagine a community's state of mind when, after a period of bloody conflict, it
is delivered from its misfortune by an unexpected mob action. In
the early days or months that followed this deliverance, it is likely
that a great euphoria prevailed. But sadly this blessed period never
lasted. Humans are so constituted that they always fall back into their
mimetic rivalries. "Scandal must occur," and it always does occur,
sporadically at first, and little attention is paid to it. But soon it begins
to proliferate. Now those affected must face facts: a new crisis threatens the community. How to prevent this disaster? The community
has not forgotten the strange, incomprehensible drama that some-
time ago drew it up from the abyss, where the community now fears it
will fall again. It is full of gratitude toward the mysterious victim who
plunged it initially into that disaster but who subsequently saved it.

When the people involved reflect on these strange events, they
must say to one another that if the whole process unfolded as it
did, it was without doubt because the mysterious victim wanted it
that way. Perhaps this god has organized this entire scenario with
the purpose of arousing his new worshipers to reproduce it and
renew its effects so that in the future they will be protected from a
possible recurrence of mimetic disorder. The idea that the gods have
instructed humans to offer them sacrifice is universal, and it is easy
to see what justifies this. Perhaps the deities want these sacrifices to
be repeated perpetually for the good of their faithful, perhaps also

for their own benefit, because they feel honored by the rituals or perhaps because the sacrificial victims nourish them.

Not knowing precisely why collective violence is such a good thing but suspecting perhaps that it is not effective only in the supernatural sphere, the communities proceed to copy their experience of violent unanimity in a fashion as exact and complete as possible. In the case of uncertainty, better to do too much than not enough. This principle explains why so many communities incorporate the mimetic crisis itself into their rituals, the crisis that set off the mimetic process of selecting the original victim.

In many sacrificial rituals, everything begins with an acting out of mimetic crisis, which is too realistic and similar to the real thing to be invented. All the subgroups quarrel and confront each other in a symmetry of opposition, which is to say "mimetically." The model can be none other than the real crisis that triggered that very process that the community tries to reproduce: unanimous violence against a victim.

So to produce its own antidote, violence must initially intensify and escalate. Many sacrificial systems certainly have a good intuition of this. Thus they consider it necessary to reproduce the crisis, without which the single victim mechanism might not be triggered. This is why so many rituals quite clearly intended to reestablish order begin with tumult of disorder, a spectacular disturbing of the peace and order of the community. This seems paradoxical, but from the mimetic perspective it is very logical.

But even if it is rational behind its apparent absurdity, this initial disorder is not universal in the rituals. Many ritual systems do not represent the initial crisis. We can easily understand why. This crisis is an unleashing of mimetic violence. If we should imitate too realistically, the risk of a total loss of control is great, and many communities refused to assume it. Probably they felt that there would always be enough disorder among them to trigger the reconciling mechanism without adding to it a supplementary acting out of violence. Even the most tumultuous rituals did not usually reproduce a mimetic crisis in all its intensity and duration. Those involved were more often content with an abbreviated and accelerated version of disorder. In other words, you don't have to jump into the fire to learn how to avoid getting burnt.

We thus understand why those offering sacrifice, almost universally, saw their sacrifices as awesome acts. They realized that the only "good violence," the violence that ends violence rather than intensifies it, is unanimous violence. They also realized that the motive force of unanimity is mimetic contagion, which increases in intensity and becomes more and more dangerous as long as it does not achieve unanimity. This is the source of the idea, universal in origin, that ritual activity is extremely dangerous. To diminish the risk, the community would try to reproduce the model as exactly and meticulously as possible.

Psychologists and psychoanalysts have fallaciously construed this concern for exactness as "neuroses," "phantasms," and other "complexes" with which they are infatuated. To a certain type of modern mind it seems obvious that religion is based on psychological illness. To dispel these modern illusions, we must discover the real action that the people offering sacrifice reproduced: the violence that is reconciling because it is spontaneously unanimous.

As ritual traditions continue through time, a period inevitably arrives when the countless repetitions "wear out" their sacrificial effectiveness. The terror that their own sacrifices inspires in the apprentice sorcerers, as the sacrificers could be called, finally disappears. It survives only in the form of comedies of terror intended to impress the uninitiated, women, and children.

A great mass of evidence, theoretical, textual, and archeological, suggests that in the beginnings of humanity the sacrificial victims were human. With the passing of time animals more and more replaced humans, but almost everywhere human communities viewed animal victims as less efficacious than human victims. In cases of extreme danger, in classical Greece, for instance, there was a reversion to human victims. If we can believe Plutarch, on the eve of the battle of Salamis Themistocles had Persian prisoners sacrificed because of pressure from the crowd. Is this so different from the miracle of Apollonius?

Chapter 7

The Founding Murder

EHIND THE PASSION OF CHRIST, behind a number of biblical dramas, behind many mythical dramas, and behind primitive rituals, we find the same process—the process of crisis and resolution founded on the same error, the same illusion. This illusion is the misunderstanding about the single victim who pays the price of the "mimetic cycle."

When we examine the great stories of origin and the founding myths, we notice that they themselves proclaim the fundamental and founding role of the single victim and his or her unanimous murder. The idea is present everywhere. In Sumerian mythology cultural institutions emerge from a single victim: Ea, Tiamat, Kingu. The same in India: the dismemberment of the primordial victim, Purusha, by a mob offering sacrifices produces the caste system. We find similar myths in Egypt, in China, among the Germanic peoples—everywhere.

The creative power of this murder is often given concrete form in the value attributed to the fragments of the victim. Each of these is identified as producing a particular institution, a totemic clan, a territorial subdivision, or even the vegetable or animal that furnishes the community its primary food. The body of the victim is sometimes compared to a seed, which must decompose in order to germinate. This germination is the same thing as the restoration of the cultural system damaged by the preceding crisis or the creation of an entirely new system, which appears often as the first one ever created, as a sort of invention of humanity. "Unless a grain of wheat falls into the ground and dies, it remains alone; but if it dies it bears much fruit" (John 12:24).

The myths presenting the founding role of the primordial murder are so numerous that even a comparative mythologist so little given to generalizations as Mircea Eliade considered it necessary to take into account. In his *Histoire des croyances et des idées religieuses*, he speaks of a "creative murder" (*meurtre créateur*) common to many stories of origin and founding myths throughout the world.[1] Here we have a theme whose frequency clearly surprises the comparative mythologist, a phenomenon that is "trans-mythological" in a way. However, in keeping with his practice of pure description, Eliade never, as far as I know, suggested the universal explanation of the theme that I think must be given.

THE THEME of the founding murder is not only mythical but also biblical. We find it in the book of Genesis, in Cain's murder of his brother, Abel. The account of this murder is not a founding myth; it is rather the biblical interpretation of all founding myths. It recounts the bloody foundation of the beginnings of culture and the consequences of this foundation, which form the first mimetic cycle narrated in the Bible.

How does Cain go about founding the first culture? The text itself does not pose this question, but it gives an answer by virtue of focusing on two themes: the first is the murder of Abel; the second is Cain as the founder of the first culture. This culture is clearly presented as the direct extension of the murder, and it cannot be distinguished from the ritual, nonvengeful developments stemming from this murder.

Their violence inspires in these murderers a salutary fear. It makes them understand the contagious character of mimetic behavior and enables them to get a glimpse of disastrous possibilities for the future. "Now that I've killed my brother," Cain says to himself, "anyone will kill me at sight" (Gen. 4:14). This last phrase, "anyone will kill me at sight," suggests that the human race is not limited at that time

---

1. Mircea Eliade, *Histoire des croyances et des idées religieuses* (Paris: Payot, 1978), 84. This book was translated into English as *A History of Religious Ideas*, trans. Willard R. Trask (Chicago: University of Chicago Press, 1978).

to Cain and his two parents, Adam and Eve. The name "Cain" designates the first community gathered around the first founding murder. This is why there are many potential murderers, and so there must be something to keep them from killing.

The founding murder teaches the murderer(s) a kind of wisdom, a form of prudence that moderates their violence. God takes advantage of the lull by promulgating the first law against murder: "If anyone kills Cain, he shall be avenged sevenfold" (Gen. 4:15). The foundation of Cainite culture is this first law against murder: each time a new murder occurs, the community will immolate seven victims in memory of the original victim, Abel. Even more than the crushing character of the retribution, it is the ritual nature of the sevenfold sacrifice that reestablishes the peace. This ritual character is rooted in the lull the original murder produced and the unanimous accord of the community in recollecting this murder.

The law against murder involves nothing other than the repetition of murder. What distinguishes it from primitive vengeance is its intention rather than the intrinsic nature of the act performed. In place of a vengeful repetition that arouses new avengers, it establishes a ritualized, sacrificial repetition of the unity forged in unanimity, a ceremony in which the entire community participates. This difference between ritual repetition and vengeful repetition may appear fine and precarious, and it is, but it is nonetheless enormously important. It bears in fact all the cultural differences to come. This first difference is the invention of human culture.

We must be careful not to read into the story of Cain a "confusion" between sacrifice and the death penalty, as if the two institutions preexisted their actual invention. The law stemming from the increase in practical wisdom that the murder of Cain produces is the common matrix of all institutions. It is the fruit of the murder of Abel. The collective murder becomes a founding murder by way of its ritual repetitions. It is not only capital punishment, the law against murder, that we should conceive as the domestication and limitation of primitive violence by means of ritual violence; it is rather all the great human institutions. As James Williams ob-

(this translator)

serves, the "sign of Cain is the sign of civilization. It is the sign of the murderer protected by God."[2]

WE FIND still other references to the founding murder in the Gospels. The idea is presupposed by two parallel passages in Matthew and Luke that mention a chain of murders similar to the Passion and going back to "the foundation of the world."

Matthew refers to the murder of prophets. Luke's text has the murder of all the prophets "since the foundation of the world," that is, "from the murder of Abel to the murder of Zechariah" (Luke 11:51). The last link of this chain is the Passion, which resembles all the previous murders. It unfolds through the same structure of mimetic escalation and the single victim mechanism.

Luke's reference to the murder of Abel is important for at least two reasons. The first is that it should discredit once and for all the narrow thesis that interprets the Gospel comments on the murders of the prophets as attacks against the Jewish people and so as manifestations of "anti-Semitism." The Jewish people did not exist in the period of Cain and Abel, and Abel is considered the first of the prophets collectively assassinated, so it is evident that the Jewish people alone could not have slain the prophets. Jesus does not wish to attack his own people. Rather Jesus emphasizes the violence of human culture. As always, his word signifies something universally human.

The second reason the reference to Abel is so important, in the context of "the foundation of the world," is that it is a return to the theme in the story of Cain in Genesis, a deliberate adoption of the thesis that I have just set out: the first human culture has its roots in an initial collective murder, a murder similar to the Crucifixion. What shows this to be so is Luke's phrase "since the foundation of the world."[3] What has happened since the foundation of the world, that is, since the violent foundation of the first cul-

---

2. James Williams, *The Bible, Violence, and the Sacred* (Valley Forge, Pa.: Trinity Press, 1995), 185.
   3. See also Matthew 13:35 and 25:34.

ture, is a series of murders like the Crucifixion. These are murders founded on violent contagion, and consequently they are murders occurring because of the collective error regarding the victim, a misunderstanding caused by violent contagion.

The two phrases in Luke suggest that the chain of murders is extremely long, going back to the foundation of the first culture. This type of murder, exemplified by the murder of Abel and the Crucifixion, plays a founding role in all of human history. It is not by accident that the Gospels connect this murder with the *katabole tou kosmou*, the foundation of the world. Luke in particular suggests that the murder has a founding character, that the first murder and the basis of the first culture are the same thing.

The Gospel of John has a saying of Jesus that is equivalent to Luke's, and it confirms the interpretation I have just given. It is a statement found in the middle of Jesus' great speech about the devil (John 8), and I have already commented on it in chapter 3. It too is a definition of that which Mircea Eliade calls the "creative" murder:

"He [the devil] was a murderer from the beginning." . . .

The word here translated "beginning" is *arche* in the Greek, which means "origin," "first appearance," or "beginning." The reference cannot be to the creation ex nihilo, for that is completely God's work and cannot be associated with violence. The "origin" or "beginning" must have to do with the first human culture. The word *arche* thus has the same sense as *katabole tou kosmou* in the Gospels of Luke and Matthew, the foundation of the first culture.

If the relation of the murder to the beginning was accidental, if it meant simply that since humans have been on the earth, Satan has driven them to murder, John wouldn't mention the word "origin" in connection with the first murder any more than Luke would connect the foundation of the world and the murder of Abel. These three phrases, two from Luke and one from John, signify the same thing: they indicate that between the origin and the first collective murder there is a relation that is not accidental. The murder and the origin are the same thing. If the devil is a murderer *from* the origin, that means that he continues to be during the rest of time. Each time a culture appears, it begins by the same type of murder. We have therefore a series of murders similar to the Passion and all founding events. If the first one is the origin of the first culture, those following must be the origin of subsequent cultures.

All this agrees perfectly with what we learned before about Satan, or the devil, namely, that he is a kind of personification of "bad contagion" just as much in its conflictive and disintegrative aspects as in its reconciling and unifying aspects. Behind all of these phases, Satan, or the devil, is the one who foments disorder, the one who sows scandals, and then at the height of the crises that he himself provokes, Satan suddenly brings them to an end by expelling the disorder. Satan expels Satan by means of innocent victims whom he succeeds in having condemned. Satan is the master of the single victim mechanism, and so he is the master of human culture, whose origin is none other than this act of murder. At the origin not only of the Cainite culture but of all human cultures is ultimately the devil, namely, the bad contagion that results in violence and is expelled thanks to the unanimous misinterpretation of the founding murder.

How BEST to interpret the idea of the founding murder? How could such an idea take specific form without appearing fantastic and even absurd?

We know that this murder acts as a kind of analgesic or tranquilizer, for when the murderers satisfy their appetite for violence on a victim who is actually irrelevant, they are sincerely convinced that they have rid their community of someone responsible for their misfortunes. But this illusion by itself is not enough to justify belief in the founding virtue of this murder. This is a belief we have just confirmed not only to be common to all the great founding myths but also to be spelled out in Genesis and finally in the Gospels.

The temporary interruption of the crisis does not suffice to explain the universal belief of so many religions in the founding power of a collective murder. Most religions believe in its power not only to found communities but also to insure an enduring and relatively stable organization of life. The reconciling effect of this murder, no matter how gripping it may be, cannot extend for generation upon generation. By itself the murder cannot produce and perpetuate cultural institutions. However, there is a satisfying answer to the question I have just asked. To discover what it is, we must appeal to the first of all human institutions after the collective murder, namely, the ritual repetition of the murder. Let us now quickly examine how thinkers have stated the question of the origin of cultural institutions and human societies.

Since the Enlightenment this question has been defined in terms that the most abstract rationalism has dictated. Rationalists conceive the first humans as so many little Descartes, who must have conceived in abstract fashion, purely theoretically at first, the institutions they wished to establish. Moving then from theory to practice, these first humans would have realized their institutional concept. Therefore no institution could exist without an *a priori* idea that guides the practical elaboration. It is this idea that determines actual cultures.

If things had really come about in this fashion, religion would have played no role in the origin of institutions. And indeed, in the context of the rationalism espoused by anthropological studies, religion plays no real part and is of absolutely no use. It can only be superfluous, superficial, a secondary addition—in other words, *superstition.* How then should one explain the universal presence of religion, supposedly so useless, right at the heart of all human institutions? When this question is asked in a rationalist context, there is only one really logical response, that of Voltaire: religion is defined as a *parasite* that attaches itself from outside to useful institutions. "Deceitful and greedy" priests invented it to exploit the credulity of good people for their own profit.

This rationalist expulsion of religion continues to dominate contemporary anthropology, even though anthropologists and other social scientists now try to conceal somewhat the simplistic character of their views. We cannot openly repudiate the rationalist bias without transforming the universal presence of sacrificial rituals in human

institutions into a formidable focal point of questioning. The modern
social sciences are essentially antireligious. If religion is not a kind
of tough weed, irritating but unimportant, what can we make of it?

Throughout history religion is the constant element in diverse
and changing institutions. Therefore we cannot discount it in favor
of the pseudo-solution that takes it as a mere nothing, the fifth
wheel of all the coaches, without coming to grips with the opposite
possibility, disagreeable as it is for modern antireligion. This possibility is that religion is the heart of every social system, the true origin
and original form of all institutions, the universal basis of human
culture.[4] This solution is all the more difficult to avoid because since
the golden days of rationalism we have learned more about ancient
societies. Among many of these societies the institutions that the
Enlightenment took for indispensable to humanity didn't yet exist:
in their place there were only sacrificial rituals.

Under the heading of rituals we can roughly distinguish three
types of societies. First there is the society in which ritual now plays
no role or almost no role, and that is contemporary society, our
society. Next there are, or used to be, societies where rituals ac-
companied institutions in some way and strengthened them. In this
case the ritual seems to be a supplement to institutions that do not
really need it. Ancient societies and, in another sense, medieval society are of this type. It is this type that early rationalist thinkers
incorrectly conceived as universal and that suggested to them the
thesis of religion as parasitic. Third and finally there are "primitive"
or "archaic" societies that do not have institutions in our sense but
that have rituals instead. They have no secular "institutions," only
rituals.

Early anthropologists used to see archaic societies as the least
evolved and the closest to human origins. In spite of attempts to
discredit their thesis, it is pointed in the right direction. However,
we cannot adopt this thesis without highlighting and pursuing the

---

4. On the strange "allergy" of modern research to all the forms of the sacred, see the fine
discussion of Cesareo Bandera at the beginning of *The Sacred Game: The Role of the Sacred in the
Genesis of Modern Literary Fiction* (University Park: Pennsylvania State University Press, 1994).

role of sacrifice. We are led to think not only that sacrifice played an essential role in the early stages of humanity but also that it could indeed have been the motivating force of all that appears to be specifically "human" in humankind. Sacrifice lies behind everything distinguishing humans from animals, behind everything enabling us to substitute properly human desire for animal instinct, namely, mimetic desire. If becoming human involves, among other things, acquiring mimetic desire, it is obvious that humans could not exist in the beginning without sacrificial institutions that repress and moderate the kind of conflict that is inevitable with the working of mimetic desire.

Many observers have noted that in exclusively ritual societies the sequences of sacrificial ritual already play the role, more or less, that will become the responsibility of subsequent institutions, which we still define according to a rationalist concept of their function. To take one example, systems of education: in the archaic world they did not exist, but "rites of passage" or rites of initiation played a role that prefigured them. Young people did not surreptitiously enter into their own cultures but they were initiated through solemn procedures in which the entire community participated. These rituals of passage include "ordeals," often quite painful, which inevitably evoke our own tests or ordeals involved in "passing" exams to get a degree, etc.

Rituals of passage or initiation, like all rituals, are based on sacrifice. Accordingly every radical change is a kind of resurrection rooted in the death that precedes it, which is the only process able to set the vital powers in motion again. In the first phase, the phase of "crisis," the initiates died, as it were, to their childhood. In the second phase they rose again, capable from now on to assume their rightful place in the world of adults. In some communities, from time to time, one of the initiates did not rise again, did not come out of the ritual ordeal alive, and this was regarded as a favorable sign for all the other initiates. Everyone saw in the one death a providential reinforcement of the sacrificial dimension of the initiation process.

To say that these rituals "replaced" our systems of education and other institutions is to put the cart before the horse. It is the modern institutions that clearly replace the rituals after having coexisted with them for a long time. All evidence suggests that sacrificial rituals came first in all areas of life in the history of humankind. There are rites of execution (the stoning prescribed in Leviticus, for example), rites of death and birth, matrimonial rites, rites of hunting and fishing in societies that pursue these activities, agricultural rites in societies dependent on agriculture, etc.

Everything we call our "cultural institutions" must stem originally from ritual acts that become so refined over the years that they lose their religious connotations and are defined in relation to the type of "crisis" they are intended to resolve. By dint of repetition the rituals are modified and transformed into practices that human reason alone seems to have worked out, whereas in reality they have a religious origin.

Sacrificial rituals are scheduled just at the moment needed when there is a crisis to resolve, and for good reason. They are initially nothing other than the spontaneous resolution of all crises by means of unanimous violence, crises that occur unexpectedly in social existence. Not solely mimetic conflicts, these crises are birth and death, changes of season, famines, disasters of all kinds, and thousands of other things besides that, right or wrong, disturb the life of primitive peoples. Human communities constantly resort to sacrifice to try to ease their distress.

ONE SUCH RESOLUTION OF CRISIS is represented in a certain kind of burial mound that we find in many areas of the world. Why do certain cultures bury their victims under heaps of stones that they often shape into a pyramid form? We can explain this custom as a by-product of ritual stonings. When a victim is stoned, the body is covered with stones. When the attackers throw a lot of stones at someone still alive, not only does the victim die, but the stones naturally take the partially conic form of a "barrow" or mound. We find just this, put more or less into geometrical form, in the sacrificial or funerary pyramids of various peoples, beginning with the Egyptians. At first the Egyptians formed the tomb as a truncated pyramid and only later built it with the full pyramid point. The burial tomb is invented beginning in that period when the custom of covering corpses with stones expanded in the absence of the stoning of victims. How do we conceive the ritual origin of political power? The origin of such power was by means of "sacred monarchy," which we should also view as a modification, minute in the beginning, of ritual sacrifice. The development of sacred kingship may be imagined in a scenario like the following.

A victim is chosen who is intelligent and commanding. Rather than sacrificing him immediately, the community, for some reason, defers his execution, which allows him to "stew in the soup" of mimetic rivalries. His fate as a future sacrifice confers religious authority on him and enables him, not to "grasp" political power, which doesn't really exist to this point, but literally to forge it. The veneration that his status as future sacrifice inspires is transformed little by little into "political" power.[5]

We can compare the ritual dimension of these institutions to a maternal substance, namely, to an original placenta, which the rituals eliminate over time as they are transformed into deritualized institutions. It is like the legend about the bear cub whom its mother formed by licking a formless little mass. The repetitions of sacrifice are like the many tongue licks needed to reach the perfect shape of a bear.

The true guide of human beings is not abstract reason but ritual. The countless repetitions shape little by little the institutions that later men and women will think they invented ex nihilo. Actually it is religion that invented human culture.

Human societies are the work of the mimetic process that has been disciplined by ritual. Human beings know very well that they cannot master mimetic rivalries by their own powers. That is why they attribute this mastery to their victims, whom they take for gods.

---

5. On the question of sacred monarchies in general and particularly in the Sudan, see Simon Simonse, *Kings of Disaster* (Leiden: E. J. Brill, 1992).

In a strictly matter-of-fact sense, they are wrong; in a deeper sense, they are right. Humanity, in my view, is the child of religion.

OUR INSTITUTIONS have to be the outcome of a slow process of secularization, which is the same thing as a sort of "rationalization," and this process suggests to the functionalists that all culture should be interpreted in terms of utility and practical implementation. Modern research would have found their true origin long ago if it had not been handicapped by its irrational hostility to religion.

We should envisage the possibility that all human institutions, and therefore humanity itself, are rooted in sacrifice. Indeed, to escape from animal instinct and arrive at mimetic desire with all its dangers of mimetic conflicts, humans have to discipline their desire, and they cannot accomplish that except by means of sacrifices. Humanity springs forth from religion, i.e., from many "founding murders" and the rituals that spring from them. The modern tendency to minimize religion could well be, paradoxically, the last remnant among us of religion itself in its archaic form, which seeks to keep the sacred at a safe distance. The trivialization of religion reflects a supreme effort to conceal what is at work in all human institutions, the religious avoidance of violence between the members of the same community.

The idea of a founding murder often passes for a bizarre invention, a recent aberration, a whim of certain modern intellectuals who are strangers just as much to common sense as to cultural realities. And yet this idea is common to the great stories of origin throughout the world, to the Bible and the Gospels. It is more likely than the various modern theories concerning the origin of societies, which all go back in one form or another to the same persistent, but implausible, idea of the "social contract."

To rehabilitate the belief of the religions that there was a founding murder and to make it scientifically plausible, we must add to this murder the cumulative effects of rituals and to take into account the plasticity of these rituals over an extremely long period of time. Turning this murder into ritual is the first institution and the most fundamental one. It is the mother of all the others, the decisive development in the invention of human culture.

The power behind the emergence of humankind is the repetition of sacrifices in a spirit of cooperation and harmony, and such cooperation and harmony are what make the sacrifices so fruitful. This thesis gives anthropology the temporal dimension missing in its approach to social origins, and it agrees with the doctrines of the religions about themselves. From the moment when the prehuman creature, the human-to-be, passed over a certain threshold of mimetic contagion and the animal instinct of protection against violence collapsed (the *dominance patterns*), mimetic conflicts must have raged among humankind, but the raging of mimetic conflict quickly produced its own antidote by giving birth to the single victim mechanism, gods, and sacrificial rituals. In spite of their own violence, the sacrificial rituals not only moderated violence but channeled it in positive, humanizing directions.

Because our desires are mimetic, they resemble each other and cluster together in systems of opposition that are obstinate, sterile, and contagious. This is how scandals come to be. As they become fewer and bigger, scandals plunge communities into crises that are inflamed more and more. This inflammation reaches the crucial moment when unanimous convergence of the community against a single victim results in a total scandal, the "abscess of fixation" that pacifies the violence and puts together again the harmony that was torn apart.

The exasperation of mimetic rivalries would have prevented human societies from forming if it had not produced its own remedy at its very height. This remedy is the single victim, or scapegoat, mechanism. Surviving in our culture in only very attenuated forms, this mechanism must have reconciled the earliest communities and given them first a ritual order and then an institutional order, which assured the community's temporal duration and a relative stability.

Yes, indeed, human societies must be the daughters of religion. *Homo sapiens* itself must be the child of the still rudimentary forms of the process I have just described.

Chapter 8

Powers and Principalities

THE PRECEDING CHAPTER has shown us that the Bible and the Gospels essentially agree with foundational myths that the cumulative effects of the "single victim mechanism" and sacrificial rituals are responsible for the foundation and development of human societies.

Christians heartily distrusted the sovereign states in which Christianity emerged and spread, on account of the violent origin of these states. In naming them Christianity did not resort to their usual names, such as the Roman Empire or the Herodian tetrarchy. Instead, the New Testament usually calls upon a specific vocabulary, that of "principalities and powers."

If we examine the Gospel and New Testament passages that speak of the powers, we confirm that implicitly or explicitly they are associated with the type of collective violence on which I have insisted. This association makes perfect sense if my thesis is right: this violence is the founding mechanism of sovereign states.

In chapter 4 of the Acts of the Apostles Peter applies a line from the second psalm to the Passion of Christ:

> The kings of the earth took their stand
> and the rulers were gathered together
> against the LORD and against his anointed.

We don't have to conclude from this quotation that Peter takes literally the participation of all "the kings of the earth" in the Crucifixion. He knows perfectly well that the Passion of Jesus didn't attract the attention of the entire world. He does not exaggerate the strictly historical importance of this event. What the quota-

95

tion means is that beyond an incident certainly minor from Rome's standpoint, Peter finds a special connection between the Cross and the powers in general because the powers are rooted in collective murders similar to what befell Jesus.

Though not identical with Satan, the powers are all his tributaries because they are all servants of the false gods that are the offspring of Satan, that is, the offspring of the founding murder. So here it is not a matter of religion for the individual or belief in a purely individual sense, as modern people tend to hold. What we are talking about here are rather the social phenomena that the founding murder created.

The system of powers Satan has engendered is a concrete phenomenon, material and simultaneously spiritual, religious in a very special sense, efficacious and illusory at the same time. It is religion as illusion, which protects humans from violence and chaos by means of sacrificial rituals. Although this system is grounded in an illusion, its action in the world is real to the extent that idolatry, or false transcendence,[1] commands obedience.

It is striking how many names the New Testament writers invent to designate these ambiguous entities. They may be called powers "of this world," then on the other hand "celestial powers," as well as "sovereignties," "thrones," "dominions," "princes of the kingdom of the air," "elements of the world," "archons," "kings," "princes of this world," etc. Why such a vast vocabulary, made up apparently of such dissimilar elements? When we examine these titles, we quickly confirm that they divide into two groups. Expressions like "powers *of this world*," "kings *of the earth*," "principalities," etc. assert the earthly character of the powers, their concrete reality here below in our world. On the other hand, expressions like "princes of the kingdom *of the air*," *celestial* powers," etc. emphasize the extraterrestrial, "spiritual" nature of these entities.

---

1. "False transcendence" is one way of indicating the outcome of the working of the single victim mechanism. The whole process of conflicting desires fixed on the model, the snowballing effect of scandal, and convergence upon the single victim leads to the establishment of institutions that are based on the error or illusion of the founding murder. — Trans.

We are talking about the same entities in both instances. The powers called "celestial" are not different at all from powers "of this world." But then why are there two groups of names? Is it because the New Testament writers don't know exactly what they mean? No, to the contrary, they are well aware, I think, that they oscillate between the two sets of terms.

The New Testament authors have an acute awareness of the twofold, ambiguous nature of these powers. What they seek to clarify is the combination of material power and spiritual power that is the sovereign reality stemming from collective, founding murders. The New Testament writers would like to name this complex reality as economically as possible, and the reason why they multiply the formulas is, I think, because the results they obtain do not satisfy them.

On the one hand, to say of the powers that they are worldly would be to dwell on their concrete reality in this world, which is an essential dimension but to the detriment of the other dimension, the religious one. Although the latter is illusory, it has effects too real to be conjured away. On the other hand, to say of the powers that they are "celestial" is to insist on their religious dimension, namely, on the prestige that thrones and sovereigns enjoy among humankind and that is always perceived as a little supernatural. We see this even now in the toadyism that bows and scurries at the feet of our governments, no matter how unimpressive the latter are. This second set of terms inevitably cancels out everything the first set brings out, and vice versa.

How can one define in one word the paradox of organizations or institutions that are very real but rooted in a transcendence that is unreal and yet effective? If the powers have many names, it is because of this paradox that constitutes them, an internal duality that human language cannot express in a simple, straightforward fashion. Human language has never assimilated what the New Testament is talking about here. It does not command the necessary resources to express the power of bringing people together that false transcendence possesses in the real, material world, in spite of its

falsity and imaginary nature. Modern readers don't understand the
problem the New Testament authors encounter, and so they gladly
read into the theme of the powers all the elements of superstition
and magical thought that they wish to find in the Gospels.

THE POWERS, though always associated with Satan and based on the
transcendence of Satan, are not "satanic" in the same sense as he is,
even though they are his tributaries. Sacrificial rituals do not seek to
become one with false transcendence; they do not aspire to mystical
union with Satan. To the contrary, they try to keep this formidable
figure at a distance and hold him at bay outside the community.

We cannot call the powers simply "diabolical," and we should not,
under the pretext that they are "evil," systematically disobey them.
It is the transcendence on which they are based that is diabolical.
The powers are never strangers to Satan, it's true, but we cannot
condemn them blindly. Moreover, in a world that is alien to the
kingdom of God, they are indispensable to the maintenance of order,
which explains the attitude of the Church toward them. St. Paul says
the powers exist because they have a role to play as authorized by
God. The apostle is too realistic to go off to war against the powers.
He recommends that Christians respect them and even honor them
as long as they require nothing contrary to Christian faith.

THE ROMAN EMPIRE is a power, even the supreme power in the world
where Christianity appears. It must therefore rest upon a founding
murder, a collective murder similar to the Passion, a kind of "lynching." At first glance this thesis appears improbable, absurd. The
argument goes that the empire had its beginning too recently and
artificially to connect it to an event so primitive as our "founding murder." And yet . . . we know the historical developments fairly
well that resulted in the basis of the Roman Empire, and we can
only confirm that they coincide admirably with the concept of this
founding basis that we find in the Gospels.

The successive emperors draw their authority from the sacrificial
power that emanates from the deity whose name they bear, the first

Caesar, who was assassinated by numerous murderers. So like every sacred monarchy, the empire is based upon a collective victim who is divinized. There is something about this so striking, so impressive, that it is impossible to see it as pure and simple coincidence. Shakespeare, who was extremely perceptive in such matters, refused to do so.

Shakespeare does not minimize this founding fact. He has an acute awareness of mimetic processes and how they are resolved, and he is an incomparable reader of the Bible. So rather than viewing the reference to Caesar's divinity as mediocre political propaganda, as so many modern historians do, the dramatist centered his tragedy of Caesar in the murder of the hero and defined quite explicitly the founding, sacrificial virtues of an event that he both connected and opposed to its counterpart in the distant past: the violent expulsion of the last king of Rome.

One of the most revealing passages is the interpretation of the sinister dream Caesar's wife has the night before the assassination. The interpreter clearly announces the founding character, or rather "re-founding" character, of this event:

> It was a vision fair and fortunate:
> Your statue spouting blood in many pipes,
> in which so many smiling Romans bathed,
> signifies that from you great Rome shall suck
> reviving blood, and that great men shall press
> for tinctures, stains, relics, and cognizance.
> (II, 2, 83–90)

The cult of the emperor explicitly reassumes the primitive scheme of the founding murder. This imperial doctrine certainly comes late in history and is too self-conscious not to include a bit of the artificial, but those who conceived it clearly knew what they were doing. They were quite successful, as the long life of the Roman Empire has proved.

We can better understand the New Testament idea of the powers if we relate it to what is still, in my view, the best of the anthropological theories of social life, Emile Durkheim's concept of "social transcendence." The great sociologist found in primitive societies a fusion of the sacred and the social that comes quite close to the basic paradox of the powers and principalities. The union of these two words, "social" and "transcendence," has been much criticized. Minds possessed by the spirit of exact science see in them a betrayal of science to the benefit of religion, while religious minds see the contrary, a betrayal of religion to the benefit of science.

Before criticizing Durkheim, we should first try to understand the effort of a thinker like him who seeks to bypass the abstractions of theorists of his time and ours. He did what he could to gain access to the problem in sociology posed by the juxtaposition of real immanence, a force arising within the social order itself, and a "transcendental" power. Although it has its roots in deception, the false transcendence of violent religion is effective as long as all the members of the community respect and obey it.

No doubt my thesis is closely related to Durkheim's concept, but I think it is going too far to define my argument as "Durkheimian." In Durkheim we find neither the mimetic cycle nor the single victim mechanism. And above all we do not find there the question I will now address, that of the insurmountable difference between primitive religions, on the one hand, and Judaism and Christianity, on the other.

Part Three

The Victory
of the Cross

Chapter 9

The Uniqueness of the Bible

U NLIKE THE OLD MODERN CRITICS, postmodern opponents of Christianity don't try to demonstrate that the Gospels and myths are similar, identical, or interchangeable. Differences don't trouble them, and in fact they pile up differences with ease. It is rather the resemblances that they suppress.

If there are only differences between the religions, they make up just one big undifferentiated conglomerate. We can no more say they are true or false than we could say a story by Flaubert or by Maupassant is true or false. To regard one of these works of fiction as more true or false than the other would be absurd. This doctrine of insignificant differences has seduced the contemporary world. Differences are the object of a veneration more apparent than real. Those who discuss religions give the impression of taking them very seriously, but in reality they don't attach the least importance to them. They view religions, all the religions, as completely mythical, but each in its own fashion. They praise them all in the same spirit we all praise kindergartners' "paintings," which are all masterpieces. The upshot of this attitude is that we are all free to buy what pleases us in the supermarket of religions, or better still to abstain from buying anything.

The old anti-Christian anthropologists knew better. Like the Christians themselves, they believed in truth. To demonstrate the Gospels were meaningless, they tried to show that they resembled myths too closely not to be mythical as well. They did, therefore, just what I have done; they sought to define what the myths and the Gospels have in common. They hoped that the two had so much in common that no room would be left for any significant difference

103

between them. In this way they tried to demonstrate the mythic character of the latter.

These industrious researchers never discovered what they were looking for, but in my view they were right to persist in their search. The reality common to foundational myths and the Gospels does exist, as I have shown: the mimetic, or "satanic," cycle. This is the three-part sequence of the initial crisis, the ensuing collective violence, and finally the religious epiphany, the "revelation" stemming from the single victim mechanism. Paradoxically, their anti-Christian perspective prevented the old anthropologists from discovering *all* the similarities between the Gospels and the myths. Fearing, no doubt, that they might fall again into the orbit of the Gospels, they kept their distance from them. They would have considered themselves disgraced if they had utilized them as I have done in the first three chapters of this book.

The Gospels are more transparent than myths, and they make everything clear around them, for they are explicit on the subject of mimetic contagion, which begins in rivalry and conflict and then becomes reconciliatory. As they reveal the mimetic process, they shed light on the obscurity of myths. If we had done the reverse and based our investigation on myths, we would learn nothing about the Gospels.

After discovering the mimetic cycle, thanks to the Gospels, we detected it again without difficulty, first in the stoning instigated by Apollonius and then in all mythic cults. From then on we knew that what keeps primitive cultures functioning is basically the regulation of the mimetic cycle, through single victim mechanisms and their ritual repetitions. The old anthropologists followed the opposite method. They believed they were obliged to find support in myths in order to attack the Gospels. They would have thought they were betraying their own cause if they had moved the other way, from the Gospels to myths.

Myths display the same mimetic process as the Gospels, of course, but usually in such an obscure and confused way that if we use them as our base and point of departure, we cannot succeed in dispelling "the darkness of Satan." My point of departure from the Gospels is not in order arbitrarily to favor Christianity and reject paganism. The discovery of the mimetic cycle in myths does not at all confirm the old Christian belief in the absolute uniqueness of Christianity and seems initially to make it more improbable and indefensible than ever. The Gospels and myths recount the same type of mimetic crisis, which is resolved by the same type of collective expulsion and concluded by an epiphany or revelation that is repeated and commemorated by rituals similar in structure. So what distinguishes mythology and Christianity in a way that confers on the latter the uniqueness it has always claimed?

In Christianity, of course, the sacrifices offered are not animals or humans. There is no longer an actual blood sacrifice. We see everywhere in Christianity the nonviolence that we observed in chapter 4, where we compared the stoning Apollonius instigated and the stoning that Christ prevented. The real Christian, however, is not content with this difference. Christianity could still appear to be an attenuated mimetic process, softened but essentially unchanged. The attenuation and mellowing appear also in a number of later mythic cults.

For the moment we can't see, at the level of the original mythic structure, what might distinguish the Gospels from myth other than in a superficial, insignificant fashion. This result would have gladdened the old anti-Christian anthropologists. For centuries the familiar feeling that Christianity is irreducibly unique was getting weaker among many Christians, and comparative anthropological studies, holding to the mythic view of Christianity, contributed to this weakening. This is, by the way, why some faithful Christians mistrust my work. They are convinced that nothing good for Christianity can come out of comparative anthropology.

THE QUESTION is so important that I am going briefly to repeat the point: when we compare a sacred revelation that the Gospels regard as false, mythical, satanic, to the sacred revelation that they regard as true, we can see no significant discrepancy. In both cases we are dealing with mimetic cycles, all of which end with scapegoats and resurrections. So what allows Christianity to define pagan religions as satanic or diabolic but to exclude itself from this definition?

I intend for this study to be as objective, as "scientific," as possible. So as you can see, I am not proposing that the Gospel opposition between God and Satan be blindly accepted. If I cannot show modern readers what makes this a real, concrete opposition, they will understandably reject it as deceptive and illusory. So for right now the two appear to be equivalent, certainly in terms of structure: the mimetic cycles that produce the mythic deities and the mimetic cycle that leads to the resurrection of Jesus and the affirmation of his divinity.

In short, the distinction between God and Satan may be an illusion produced by the desire of Christians to view their religion as unique and to proclaim themselves as the sole adherents of a truth that is alien to mythology. Not only non-Christians but also many Christians, aware of resemblances between the Gospels and the myths, deny the Christian claim of uniqueness today.

The mimetic cycle in the Gospels contains the three phases of the mythic cycles: crisis, collective violence, and sacred revelation. Nothing objectively distinguishes it from a myth. Is it not merely one more myth of death and resurrection, a little more refined perhaps than many others, but fundamentally similar?

RATHER THAN DEALING with this problem directly, I will divide it into two parts. In doing so, I will draw upon the book to which true Christians are as devoted as to the New Testament, the book they call the Old Testament, the Hebrew Bible. For tactical reasons that will become evident as we go, I will begin with the Old Testament, and this apparent detour will lead me into the heart of my subject.

The theme common to both myth and Gospel is the mimetic cycle, and it is found only partially in the Old Testament accounts. The mimetic crisis and collective violence are there, but the third phase of the mimetic cycle is absent: the sacred revelation, the resurrection that reveals the divinity of the victim. To repeat, only the first two phases are present in the Hebrew Bible. It is quite evident in these texts that the victims never rise again: God is never victimized, nor is the victim divinized.

Thus between the Hebrew Bible and the myths there is this difference, one extremely significant for the problem that occupies us. In biblical monotheism we cannot suspect God of being the product of the scapegoat processes that quite visibly produce the gods in primitive polytheism.

Now we will compare a great biblical account, the story of Joseph, to the most well-known myth of all, the story of King Oedipus. The results will facilitate our access to the essential problem, the divinity of Jesus Christ in the Christian religion. Let's verify at the outset that the first two phases of the mimetic cycle—the crisis and the collective violence—do occur in both our texts.

The myth and the biblical account both commence with the *childhood* of the two heroes. In both cases, this first part narrates a crisis within the two families, which is resolved by the violent expulsion of the two heroes while they are yet children (Oedipus is still a baby).

In the myth an oracle precipitates the crisis between the parents and their newborn son. The divine voice announces that Oedipus will someday kill his father and marry his mother. Seized with fright, Laius and Jocasta decide to slay their son. Oedipus barely escapes death but is expelled from his own family.

In the biblical story the jealousy of the ten brothers precipitates the crisis. The point of departure is different, but the result is the same. The ten want to kill Joseph, but finally they sell him as a slave to a caravan heading for Egypt. Just like Oedipus, in short, Joseph barely escapes death and is expelled from his own family.

In the parallel beginnings we recognize what we expected to find, a mimetic crisis and a single victim mechanism. In both instances a community gathers unanimously against one of its members and violently expels him. In the course of the two stories there is a second crisis, which is followed by a second expulsion in the case of Oedipus.

Oedipus escapes the claws of the Sphinx by resolving her enigma, and in solving the puzzle he also saves the entire city. The city of Thebes rewards him by making him its king. But the victory is not final. Some years later, unknown to all including the hero, the predictions of the oracle come to pass. Oedipus killed his father and married his mother. To prevent the Thebans from sheltering in their midst a son who is both parricidal and incestuous, Apollo strikes them with a plague that compels them to expel Oedipus a second time.

Let us return to Joseph. To extricate himself from his predicament in Egypt, this hero makes good use of the same kind of talent as Oedipus, the deciphering of riddles. He interprets dreams, those of two royal officials initially, then Pharaoh's himself, the famous dream of the seven fat cows and the seven lean cows. His gift of clairvoyance gets our hero released from prison (imprisonment amounted to an expulsion) and protects Egypt from the consequences of the famine. Pharaoh raises Joseph to the rank of prime minister. His wonderful talent propels him to the top of the social ladder, exactly like Oedipus.

Because of the initial expulsions, Oedipus and Joseph both have to become foreigners and are thus always a little suspect in the principal place where they perform their exploits: Thebes for Oedipus, Egypt for Joseph. The careers of these two heroes follow an alternating course of brilliant achievements and violent expulsions. Consequently, between the myth and the biblical story the numerous and essential similarities confirm our previous finding. We always find the mimetic processes of crises and violent expulsions in mythical as well as in biblical texts.

The myth and the biblical account are much closer to one another and resemble each other much more than most readers suspect. Is this to say they agree on everything essential? Can we view them as more or less equivalent? Completely to the contrary. Locating the common data allows us to take note of an irreducible difference, an impassable gulf between the biblical story and the myth.

The myth and the biblical story are in basic opposition over the decisive question that collective violence poses: Is it warranted? Is it legitimate? In the myth the expulsions of the hero are justified each time. In the biblical account they never are. Collective violence is unjustifiable.

Laius and Jocasta have good reason to rid themselves of a son who, at some point in the future, will kill the one and marry the other. The Thebans also have good reason to rid themselves of their king. Oedipus really committed the infamous acts the oracle prophesied, and to top it all he gave the plague to the whole city! In the myth, the victim is always wrong, and his persecutors are always right.

The reverse is true in the Bible: Joseph is in the right against his brothers as well as the next two times against the Egyptians, who imprison him. He is in the right against the wanton wife who accused him of trying to rape her. Potiphar, Joseph's master, treats his young slave as though he's really his son, and so the accusation raised against Joseph recalls the accusation of incest made against Oedipus. There we see one more element the two accounts have in common, but as in all the other instances the structural similarity is the basis of a radical difference from the standpoint of the narrative's identification with the victim. The mythic perspectives, and the modern theories that prolong them (psychoanalysis, for example), take the mythic accusation for legitimate. In our eyes everyone is more or less guilty of parricide and incest, if only at the level of desire. The biblical story refuses to take this kind of accusation seriously. It recognizes in it the typical obsession of hysterical crowds against those whom they make their victims for the least thing. Not only did Joseph not have sex with the wife of Potiphar, but he did everything he could to resist her advances. She is the guilty one, and behind her the Egyptian crowd, like dumb cattle following the herd in the expulsions of young immigrants who are isolated and without means or political pull.

The relation of the two heroes to the two scourges that strike their adopted countries repeats and recapitulates both the multiple convergences of the two texts and, above all, the single divergence that is absolutely decisive. Oedipus is responsible for the plague and can do nothing to heal it short of his own expulsion. But Joseph is not responsible for the famine. Moreover, he manages the crisis so ably that he protects Egypt from the disaster that could have occurred.

The same question underlies both narratives: does the hero deserve to be expelled? The myth answers at every point "yes," and the Bible answers "no," "no," and "no." The career of Oedipus ends in an expulsion whose finality confirms his guilt. Joseph's career ends in a triumph whose finality confirms his innocence.

The fundamental nature of the contrast between the myth and the biblical account suggests that the latter is the expression of an antimythological inspiration. And this inspiration discloses something essential in the myths that would remain invisible outside of the perspective the biblical narrative represents. The myths always condemn all victims, who are isolated and overwhelmed. They are the work of agitated crowds that are incapable of identifying and criticizing their own tendency to expel and murder those who cannot defend themselves, scapegoats that they always take for guilty of the same stereotypical crimes: parricide, incest, bestial fornication, and other horrible misdeeds whose perpetual and improbable recurrence point up their absurdity.

IN THE EPISODE that follows, a moment of reckoning occurs between Joseph and his brothers, one that is peaceful in keeping with Joseph's affirmation of God's providential intentions for Israel and Egypt (Gen. 45:1–15). The story of Joseph continues beyond this episode, but it is the real conclusion of the main plot of Joseph sold by his brothers and expelled by his own family that concerns us here. It confirms in unequivocal fashion, as we shall see, the biblical opposition to mythic collective violence.

The seven years of lean cows have begun, and the ten half-brothers of Joseph suffer because of the famine in Canaan. So they travel to Egypt to beg for food. They don't recognize Joseph as prime minister in his beautiful garments, but Joseph recognizes them. Without making himself known, he inquires discreetly about Benjamin, their younger brother, whom they left at home for fear that some misfortune would happen to him and their old father, Jacob, would die of grief.

Joseph gives wheat to all his half-brothers. He warns them, however, that if they come back because of the famine, they must bring Benjamin, or they will get nothing. The famine continues on, so the ten finally return to Egypt. This time they have Benjamin with them. Joseph allows them to buy wheat, but he also has a servant conceal a precious cup in Benjamin's sack. Complaining then that someone stole this article from him, Joseph has their bags searched. When the cup is found, he announces the arrest of the allegedly guilty brother, Benjamin, and he authorizes the ten older brothers to return home peacefully.

In short, Joseph submits his guilty brothers to a temptation they know well since they have already succumbed to it, that of abandoning with impunity their youngest brother, the weakest and most vulnerable among them. Nine of the brothers fall a second time to this temptation. Only Judah resists it and offers himself in the place of Benjamin. In recompense for Judah's willingness to replace Benjamin, Joseph weeps and pardons all the brothers. In his adopted country he welcomes and receives his entire family, including his old father, Jacob.

This final episode is a meditation on the kind of collective violence with which the biblical story is obsessed just as much as the myths, but the results are just the reverse. The final triumph of Joseph is, not an insignificant "happy ending," but a means of making explicit the problem of violent expulsions. Without ever leaving its narrative framework the biblical account pursues a reflection on violence whose radicalism is revealed at the point where pardon replaces the obligatory vengeance. It is only this pardon, this forgiveness, that is capable of stopping once and for all the spiral of reprisals, which of course are sometimes interrupted by unanimous expulsions, but violently and only temporarily. The biblical account accuses the ten brothers of hating Joseph for no good reason and of envying him because of his intrinsic superiority and their father

Jacob's doting on him. The real cause of the expulsion is mimetic rivalry.

This § (112-15) v. defensive

COULD ANYONE accuse me of slanting my analysis in favor of my position and of the biblical story? I believe not.

If the myth and the biblical account were both fictional works, the production of fantasy, "stories" in the sense of postmodern criticism, their disagreement about the guilt or innocence of the two victims, Oedipus and Joseph, might not mean anything at all. The differences might well have their roots in the individual caprice of the two authors, in the preference of the one for stories that have an "unhappy ending" and of the other for stories that have a "happy ending." All texts are comparable to the forever changing Proteus, postmodern critics repeat unceasingly, so the interpreter cannot reduce them to one constant theme.

Always happy to kill off any meaning, our deconstructors and other postmodern intellectuals will certainly not want to grant that the myths and the biblical texts embody two opposing positions on the question of collective violence. My response to the objection is that the biblical narrative's refusal to accept the expulsions of Joseph cannot be accidental. It could be none other than a deliberate critique of the mythic attitude, not only because of the last episode of the Joseph story but also because this story is narrated in the context of all the data that are common to mythic and biblical texts. It is these data that I analyzed at length in the previous chapters before finding them again in our two stories. We find there a web of correspondences too tight to be accidental. The multiple similarities guarantee the significance of the single but decisive difference. A thoroughgoing refusal of mythic expulsions: this is what the biblical account teaches us.

The comparison of the myth and the story of Joseph shows that the biblical author probably intended to criticize, not the myth of Oedipus specifically, but one or several unidentifiable myths that must have been similar to the Oedipus myth. The biblical story condemns the general tendency of myths to justify collective violence, which is part and parcel of the accusatory, vindictive nature of foundational myths.

We must not think of the relation between myth and the Bible in terms of the sole difference in perspective on victims and executioners, nor must we think of this relation in terms of similarities only. To arrive at the true meaning, we must focus on the difference in the context of all the similarities.

In myths as in the biblical text the expulsions of individuals adjudged to be evildoers play a huge role. Both myth and biblical text agree on this point, but the myths are incapable of criticizing this role; they cannot question themselves about collective expulsion as such. The biblical account, on the other hand, attains this level of questioning and resolutely affirms the injustice of collective expulsion.

So the discovery of all the features common to the myth of Oedipus and the story of Joseph, the presence of the mimetic cycle in such texts, does not at all demonstrate the equivalence of these two texts. It allows us rather to dismiss the trifling and useless differences of contemporary postmodern "differentialism,"[1] which can do nothing but multiply differences that lead further and further into absurdity. In avoiding this obsession with difference, we can concentrate on the essential divergence of what has to be called biblical *truth* from the *lie* of mythology.

This truth transcends the question of referentiality in the biblical account. That is, does it refer to real events outside the story or not? The essential truth of the Joseph story lies, not in its possible correspondence to facts outside the text, but in its critique of mythic expulsions. This critique is absolutely relevant given that these expulsions always have their source in mimetic contagion and thus are not the fruit of rational, impartial judgment.[2]

---

1. Differences are essential to language and culture, a principle that structuralist thinkers first articulated systematically. Postmodern critics like Derrida took over the principle of opposition and difference from structuralists, for example, Lévi-Strauss's anthropological studies of "the raw and the cooked," and turned it into a dogma that says there is no foundation or essence or truth, just simply differences, oppositions that continually undercut one another. — Trans.

2. This does not mean I assume that the story of Joseph must be imaginary or fictional. I am saying only that even if it were, it would still be more *true* than the myth of Oedipus.

Far from being minor, the divergence of the biblical account and the myth of Oedipus, or whatever other myth, is so great that no greater difference could exist. It's the difference between a world where arbitrary violence triumphs without being recognized and a world where this same violence is identified, denounced, and finally forgiven. It's the difference between truth and deception, both of them absolute. Either we succumb to the contagion of the mimetic snowballing effect and fall into the lie of victimization, with mythology, or we resist this contagion and rise into the truth of the innocent victim, with the Bible.

The story of Joseph is a refusal of the religious illusions of paganism. It discloses a universal human truth that is relative neither to the referentiality or nonreferentiality of the story nor to a system of beliefs nor to a historical period nor to language nor to cultural context. It is therefore absolute. And yet it is not a "religious" truth in the strict sense of the term.

Does the story of Joseph show partiality to the young Israelite separated from his people, isolated among the Gentiles? Even if one conceded to Nietzsche and Marx that the biblical narratives consistently favor the victims, especially if they are Jewish, it is still not appropriate to place the Bible and the myths on the same level on the pretext that their contrasting prejudices are equivalent. They are not.

The Jewish people, tossed from expulsion to expulsion, are certainly well placed to put the myths in question and to detect in them more quickly than many other peoples the scapegoat phenomena of which they are often the victims. They demonstrate exceptional discernment in the matter of persecutory crowds and their tendency to close ranks against foreigners, those who are isolated, the crippled, the disabled of all sorts. This advantage, gained at a high price throughout history, does nothing to diminish the universality of the biblical truth, nor does it permit us to take this truth as relative.

Neither the resentment that Nietzsche consistently invoked nor Jewish "chauvinism" or "ethnocentrism" could have produced the story of Joseph. The Bible refuses to demonize or deify the victims of violent crowds. The ones really responsible for expulsions are not the victims but their persecutors, the crowds or mobs caught up in mimetic contagion, such as envious brothers and Egyptians who blindly accept false accusations.

We are not foundering in dogmatism, fanaticism, or ethnocentrism if we recognize the kind of truth characteristic of biblical narrative. We demonstrate real objectivity. Not long ago in our society the word "myth" was a synonym of "lie." Our intelligentsia has done everything it could since then to rehabilitate the myths at the expense of the Bible, but in ordinary speech "myth" continues to mean lie. Ordinary speech is right.

ALL THE VICTIMS in the Bible do not have as much good fortune as Joseph; they don't always succeed in escaping their persecutors and in turning away persecution to improve their fate. More often than not they perish. These victims are alone, abandoned by all, encircled by numerous and powerful persecutors, and so their persecutors crush them. The story of Joseph is happy and "optimistic" in that the victim defeats his enemies. Other biblical accounts, on the other hand, seem "pessimistic," but that does not keep them from witnessing to the same truth as the Joseph story and opposing the mythical perspective in exactly the same way.

What gives the Bible its specific character does not consist in painting reality in cheerful colors and minimizing the power of evil. It consists rather in *interpreting* with objectivity the mimetic war of all against one, in identifying the role played by mimetic contagion in a world where there are still only myths. In the biblical world human beings are generally just as violent as in the mythic worlds, and single victim mechanisms abound. What stands against any world of contagion and violence is the Bible itself, the biblical interpretation of these phenomena.

WHAT IS TRUE of the story of Joseph is also true in the diverse forms used by narrators of many of the psalms. As far as I know, these texts are the first in human history to allow those who would simply become silent victims in the world of myth to voice their complaint as hysterical crowds besiege them. Human packs pursue them, insult them rudely, set traps for them, and encircle them in order to lynch them.

These victims are not silent: they curse their persecutors loud and long. They express their anguish with an energetic and picturesque forcefulness that scandalizes and irritates crowds more modern than those of the psalms, particularly those made up of politically correct readers. Our countless professors of compassion deplore the lack of polite speech that these speaker-victims use regarding their lynchers. The only violence that scandalizes these professional redressers of wrong is the purely verbal violence of victims at the point of being lynched.

As for the real physical violence of the executioners themselves, our puritans of violence don't seem to see it, taking it for null and void of meaning. Some other puritans of violence taught them that only texts are violent. What is essential concerning human violence escapes them. They have completely given themselves over to the antirealistic school of reading texts. Our modern methods of criticism have taken that course. They have suppressed, hidden, or eliminated the "referent," which is to say what the psalms are really about. These critics in consternation about "the violence of the psalms" are in my view completely and totally mistaken. They don't see the most important point. They give no attention to the only violence worthy of being taken seriously, the violence about which the narrators complain. They suspect nothing of the extraordinary originality of the psalms, which may be the oldest texts in human history to let the voice of the victims, rather than that of their persecutors, be heard.

The situations that these psalms present are just as mythic as the story of Joseph. But they make us think of someone who has the intriguing idea of wearing a magnificent fur inside out; rather than radiating luxury, composure, and sensuality, this one's appearance is just the reverse: we see evidence of an animal skinned alive. This metaphor forces us to understand the difference between a myth and a biblical psalm.

THE BOOK OF JOB is, in effect, an immense psalm, and its uniqueness lies in its confrontation with two conceptions of God. The pagan conception is that of the crowd who long venerated Job but who all at once, by an inexplicable, purely mimetic whim, turned against him. This conception sees the will of God in the crowd's unanimous hostility, just as in its idolatry before. The crowd's hostility is the irrefutable proof that Job is guilty and must confess his guilt. The crowd takes itself for God, and its agents are the three "friends" it has delegated to go to him. Through the friends the crowd, as it terrorizes the accused, tries to obtain his mimetic assent to the verdict that condemns him, just as in the totalitarian trials of the twentieth century that regress to the old paganism with its mechanism of unanimous persecution and expulsion in order to resolve contagion turning into violence.

Job as "super-psalm" shows in an admirable way that the sacred and the crowd are the same thing in mythic cults. This is why the primordial expression of the mythic cult is sacrificial lynching, the Dionysian dismemberment of the victim. What is most important in the book of Job is, not the murderous conformity of the multitude, but the final audacity of the hero himself, whom we see hesitate at length, vacillate, then finally take hold of the mimetic contagion and defeat it. In doing this, Job not only resists totalitarian contagion but wrests the deity out of the process of persecution to envision him as the God of victims, not of persecutors. This is what Job means when he affirms, "As for me, I know that my Defender lives" (19:25).

In all these texts the ones in the right are not the executioners, as in the myths, but the victims. The victims are innocent, and the executioners are guilty, guilty of persecuting innocent victims.

The Bible demonstrates a skepticism regarding mimetic violence, one that never before had been able to insinuate itself into a spiritual universe where the massive, irresistible character of the mythic illusion protected primitive societies from any destabilizing knowledge.

It's not accurate to say that the Bible *reestablishes* a truth that the myths betrayed. If we did, we would give the impression that this truth was already accessible, at human disposal before the Bible discovered it. No, not at all. Before the Bible there were only myths. No one and no tradition before the Bible were capable of calling into question the guilt of victims whom their communities unanimously condemned. *i.e. within known history (prehistory being by definiti inaccessib*

The reversal of the relation of innocence and guilt between victims and executioners is the keystone of biblical inspiration. It is not one of those binary polarities, nice and pretty but insignificant, which give great delight to structural anthropologists: the raw and the cooked, the hard and the soft, the sugared and the salted. No, here the most crucial problem is set before us: human relations continually disturbed by mimetic rivalry.[3]

Once we apprehend the biblical criticism of mimetic contagion and its results, we can understand the biblical profundity of the talmudic principle that Emmanuel Lévinas often cites: "If everyone is in agreement to condemn someone accused, release him for he must be innocent." Unanimity in human groups is rarely a vehicle of truth; more often it is nothing but a mimetic, tyrannical phenomenon. It resembles unanimous elections in totalitarian countries. *What abt Quaker mtgs? Ecumenical Councils?*

IN MYTHS the real reasons that impel the persecutors to deify their victim are concealed, but in the Joseph story these reasons can be surmised when the ten brothers come before their victim, who now has an air of royal splendor.

When the ten brothers expelled Joseph, they must have been tempted to demonize him. When they finally recognize him in Egypt, they must be tempted to deify him. He is a living god, after all,

---

3. On the relation of all this to the humanities and social sciences, see François Lagarde, *René Girard ou la christianisation des sciences humaines* (New York: Peter Lang, 1994), as well as Lucien Scubla, *Lire Lévi-Strauss* (Paris: Odile Jacob, 1998).

like Pharaoh, to whom Joseph is as close as possible. However, the ten brothers resist the temptation to idolatry. They are Israelites, and so they don't deify human beings. Mythic heroes typically have something rigid and stylized about them. They are first demonized, then deified. Joseph is humanized. The narrator bathes him in a warm luminosity that would be unthinkable in mythology. But this is not basically due to "literary talent," for the genius of the text is its renunciation of idolatry.

The refusal to deify victims is inseparable from another aspect of the biblical revelation, the most important of all: the deity is no longer victimized. For the first time in human history the divine and collective violence are separated from one another. The Bible rejects the gods created by sacralized violence. In certain biblical texts, particularly in the historical books, there are residues of sacred violence, but these are vestiges without a future.

The criticism of collective contagion is a criticism of the mecha-nism producing the gods. The single victim mechanism is a purely human abomination. That does not mean that the divine disappears or is weakened. What characterizes the biblical tradition is above all the discovery of a divine reality that no longer belongs to the sphere of the collective idols of violence.

This divine reality does not get weaker in separating itself from violence; it acquires more significance than ever in the person of the one God, Yahweh, who encompasses all divinity and does not depend at all on what happens among humankind. This is the God who reproaches humans for their violence and has compassion on their victims. Yahweh substitutes the sacrifice of animals for the firstborn sons and later objects even to animal sacrifices.

The Bible, in revealing the single victim mechanism, enables us to understand the type of world that polytheism projects. It appears superficially more harmonious than ours because ruptures in the harmony are generally resolved by triggering a single victim mecha-nism and the emergence of a new god, who prevents the victim from appearing as a victim.

The indefinite multiplication of primitive and pagan gods looks like an amiable fantasy to many in our time, something created for no serious reason—playful, we might say, or rather "ludic," since the word is à la mode. It is a playful fantasy of which an overly serious monotheism, not playful at all, tries to deprive us. In reality, however, the primitive and pagan gods are not playful; they are mournful and destructive. Before placing too much confidence in Nietzsche, our era should have meditated on one of the most sharp and brilliant sayings of Heraclitus: "Dionysos is the same thing as Hades." Dionysos, in other words, is the same thing as hell, the same thing as Satan, the same thing as death, the same thing as the lynch mob. Dionysos is the destructiveness at the heart of violent contagion.

Chapter 10

The Uniqueness of the Gospels

T O SUMMARIZE THE MAIN POINT about the Bible and mythology: in the myths an irresistible contagion compels the unanimous communities to see their victims first as guilty and later as divine. The divine stems from the deceptive unanimity of persecution. In the Bible, by contrast, the confusion of the victimization process and the divine is dissolved and gives way to an absolute separation of the two. As already noted, the Jewish religion no longer turns victims into divinities or divinity into a victim. Monotheism is both the cause and the consequence of this revolution.

Then in the Gospels once again we find not only the first two stages of the mimetic cycle but also the third, which the Jewish Scriptures dramatically rejected: the divinity of the collective victim. The resemblances between Christianity and the myths are too close not to awaken the suspicion of a fall back into the mythical.

Jesus is a collective victim, and Christians see him as the one true God. How do we avoid the conclusion that the affirmation of his divinity has any other cause than that of the mythic deities?

It is likely that from the beginnings of humankind all the gods grow out of the single victim mechanism. Judaism conquered this Hydra with a thousand heads. The originality of the Hebrew Bible in relation to the myths is obvious, and it appears to be annulled by the divinity of Jesus.

The Christian commitment to the one and only God not only does not resolve everybody's doubts; it often reinforces them. To reconcile the divinity of the biblical Yahweh with the divinity of Jesus, as well as with the Holy Spirit, to whom the Gospel of John explicitly ascribes a role in the redemptive process, the theology of the great ecumenical councils elaborated the concept of the one God as a *Trinity*. This concept comes across to Judaism as the return of polytheism, now badly disguised. The Muslims also, defining themselves as "strict monotheists," are quite clear that in their eyes Christians are lax monotheists, at the very least.

The same goes for all those who observe Christianity from the outside. From a philosophical, scientific, or even religious perspective, the religion that proclaims the divinity of Jesus Christ gives the impression of being nothing other than a myth that diverse influences have modified but that is not essentially different from the ancient myths of death and resurrection.

Christian dogma has always inspired distrust in Judaism and Islam, and nowadays many Christians are beginning to share that attitude. The Cross appears too strange to them, too outdated, to be taken seriously. How could one believe that a young Jew, killed nearly two thousand years ago by a type of torture long since abolished, could be the incarnation of the Almighty God?

Christianity has been losing ground for centuries in the Western world, a decline that continues to accelerate. Now not only isolated individuals abandon the churches, but entire churches, led by their clergy, switch their allegiance and go over to the camp of "pluralism." This pluralism is a relativism that claims it is "more Christian" than the adherence to dogma because it is "kinder" and more "tolerant" toward non-Christian religions.

FROM THE PERSPECTIVE of a "strict" monotheism, therefore, Christianity gives the impression of falling back into mythology: once again the single victim mechanism seems to become the source of the divine. But from my anthropological perspective we can verify that the Gospels maintain the essential victory the Bible achieves, for the relation between victims and persecutors in the Gospels bears no resemblance at all to that of the myths. It is the biblical relation that prevails, the relation we have just discovered in the story of Joseph: just like the Hebrew Bible, the Gospels defend the victims wrongly accused and expose their persecutors.

Jesus is innocent, and those who crucify him are guilty. John the Baptist is innocent, and those who have him decapitated are guilty. The continuity between the Jewish Bible and the New Testament is real and substantial. The refusal to follow Marcion, who wanted to separate the Gospels and the Hebrew Bible, is based on this continuity. Christian orthodoxy affirms that the two testaments are united as part of one and the same revelation.

We can well explain the mythic deification of victims by the working of the mimetic cycle, as we have seen. The deification process is based on the capacity of victims to polarize violence, bringing the community together as it transfers its mimetic contagion to the victim. The victim enables the "abscess of fixation" to function, which reabsorbs and pacifies all the conflicts. If the transference that demonizes the victim is powerful enough, then the reconciliation is so sudden and complete that it appears to be miraculous and triggers a second transference superimposed on the first one, the transference of deification.

There is no prior demonization behind the divinity of Christ. Christians don't ascribe any guilt to Jesus. Thus his divinity cannot rest on the same process as mythic deifications. Moreover, contrary to what happens in the myths, it is not the unanimous mob of persecutors who see Jesus as the Son of God and God himself; it is a rebellious minority, a small group of dissidents that separates from the collective violence of the crowd and destroys its unanimity. This minority group is the community of the first witnesses to the Resurrection, that is, the apostles and those who gather around them. This dissident minority has no equivalent in the myths. Around the mythic deities we never see the community divide into two unequal groups, of which only the smaller one would proclaim the divinity of the god. The structure of the Christian revelation is unique.

The Gospels are revelatory in the same way as the great biblical narratives. But even more than this, they go still further in exposing the mythic illusion. We can verify this at several levels.

The violent contagion that the myths don't reveal at all is exactly what the story of Joseph and other biblical texts do reveal to us. They describe it with one word when the narrator accuses the brothers of Joseph of "jealousy," for example. The Gospels add to this word the extensive developments that I treated in the early chapters. The word "scandal" articulates for the first time mimetic conflict and its consequences. The figure of Satan, or the devil, is even more revealing: it articulates not only all that scandal does, but beyond that it expresses the generative power of mimetic contagion with regard to mythic religion. Nowhere in the world, even in our time, can we find this description of the mimetic war of all against one and its effects as complete as the Gospels give. Moreover, they contain unique information about what makes this disclosure possible.

In order for a single victim mechanism to be described in a precise and truthful fashion, it must first occur, and in order to occur, it must be unanimous or near-unanimous. This is indeed what we find at first in the Passion accounts, thanks to the failures of the disciples. Then there must be a rupture of this unanimity just small enough not to destroy its mythic effect but sufficient all the same to assure the revelation that will come and the mission of spreading it throughout the world. This is what occurs in the case of the Crucifixion.

These requirements must be fulfilled as well in the case of the Old Testament, in the narratives that display the mechanism of violent unanimity. These accounts, however, do not contain any direct information on that point. We can speculate that the notion of a faithful *remnant* must apply to dissenting minorities similar to the group of the apostles in the Gospels. However, the Gospel accounts are the only texts in which the rupture of unanimity comes about, as it were, before our eyes. This rupture is part of the revelation. It is so much more striking that it occurs, as I said, after the failures of the disciples, after the remarkable demonstration of the extreme power of violent contagion even over the apostles, in spite of the teachings and warnings of Jesus.

The four narratives of the Passion enable us to see the effects of mimetic snowballing not only on the Jewish and Roman authorities but also on the two men crucified with Jesus and even on the

But they differ.

disciples themselves. That is to say, the mimetic escalation affected all the witnesses, without exception. (Only a few women are not affected, but their witness does not carry the weight of authority in the historical setting.)

Thus the Gospels reveal the full and complete truth about the origin of myth, about the illusory power of mimetic snowballing, about everything that the myths do not and cannot reveal because they are duped by it. This is why I began this book with the explanation of ideas drawn from the Gospels: the imitation of Christ, the concept of scandal, and the concept of Satan. Only there could I obtain what I needed to show that the Gospel notion of revelation is not at all an illusion or fraud, but a formidable anthropological reality.

Most astonishing of all, the Resurrection and the Christian divinization of Jesus correspond exactly, at the structural level, to the mythic divinization of victims whose falsity the Gospels reveal. Far from transforming or deforming or falsifying or hiding the mimetic process of the myths, the resurrection of Christ sheds the light of truth on everything that had always been concealed from human beings. Only the Resurrection, because it enlightens the disciples, reveals completely the things hidden since the foundation of the world, which are the same thing as the secret of Satan, never disclosed since the origin of human culture: the founding murder and the origin of human culture.

The Gospel revelation alone has permitted us to succeed in reaching a coherent interpretation of myth and ritual and of human culture in its entirety. I have devoted the first two parts of this book to that work.

THE RESURRECTION OF CHRIST crowns and finishes both the subversion and the unmasking of mythology, of archaic ritual, of everything that insures the foundation and perpetuation of human cultures. The Gospels reveal everything that human beings need to understand their moral responsibility with regard to the whole spectrum of violence in human history and to all the false religions.

In order for the single victim mechanism to work, as we have seen, their own contagious escalation and the battle of all against one must not be understood by the participants. The mythic process is based on a certain *ignorance* or even a *persecutory unconscious* that the myths never identify since it possesses them. The Gospels disclose this unconscious not only in the Gospel of John's portrayal of a humanity trapped in the lies of the devil but in several explicit definitions of the persecutory unconscious. The most important of these we find in the Gospel of Luke, the famous prayer of Jesus during the Crucifixion: "Father, forgive them because they don't know what they are doing" (23:34).

Here, as with all the sayings of Jesus, it is crucial to avoid emptying what he says of its basic sense by reducing it to a rhetorical formula, to a kind of sentimental exaggeration, for example. We should always take Jesus at his word. He expresses the powerlessness of those caught up in the mimetic snowballing process to see what moves and compels them. Persecutors think they are doing good, the right thing; they believe they are working for justice and truth; they believe they are saving their community.

We find the same theme in the Acts of the Apostles, also the work of the author of Luke, but in a less striking style. Peter, speaking to those involved in the crucifixion of Jesus, grants them the benefit of extenuating circumstances by virtue of what he calls their *ignorance:*

> "Now I know, brothers, that you acted out of ignorance, just as your leaders did." (Acts 3:17)

What is true of the collective mechanism also holds for mimetic occurrences between individuals. Scandals are above all a kind of inability to see, an insurmountable blindness. The First Epistle of John defines them by the darkness that spreads about them:

> Whoever says he is in the light,
> yet hates his brother,
> is still in the darkness.

> Whoever loves his brother remains in the light,
> and there is no scandal in him. (1 John 2:9–10)

Duping oneself is what characterizes the entire satanic process, and that is why one of the titles of the devil, as I have already mentioned, is "prince of darkness." In revealing the self-deception of those who engage in violence, the New Testament dispels the lie at the heart of their violence. It spells out everything we need to reject our own mythic view of ourselves, our belief in our own innocence.

THE GOSPELS are well aware of what they are doing. They not only tell the truth about victims unjustly condemned, but they know they are telling it, and they know that in speaking the truth they are taking again the path of the Hebrew Bible. The Gospels understand their kinship with the ancient Scripture regarding the single victim mechanism, and they borrow from it some of its most striking formulations.

As I have noted, the narrators of certain psalms are threatened with collective violence. Jesus recognizes and denounces a mimetic contagion of the same type as that which the narrator of this or that psalm had suffered. If we recognize that we are dealing with the same process in both cases, the Gospels' frequent recourse to the Jewish Bible becomes clear.

A typical example in the Gospel of John is the way Jesus, soon to be crucified, cites a very simple saying, "They hated me without cause" (John 15:25; cf. Ps. 35:19). It appears banal at first, but this sentence expresses the essential nature of the hostility against the victim. The hostility is without any specific reason precisely because it is the poisoned fruit of mimetic contagion rather than rational motives, or even real feeling among the individuals who feel it. Long before Jesus, the victim who speaks to us in the psalm understood the absurdity of this hatred. It is not at all an exaggeration, and so the expression "without cause" should be taken literally.

The narrators of the psalms comprehend that the crowd chooses them as victims for motives that are foreign not only to justice but also to any rational motivation. The crowd does not have a truly personal motive to lay blame on the victim it selects rather than on some other individual. It has no grievance, legitimate or illegitimate. In a society that has fallen prey to anarchy the voracious appetite for persecution feeds on victims indiscriminately, as long as they are weak and vulnerable. The least pretext is enough. No one really cares about the guilt or innocence of the victim.

These two words, *without cause,* marvelously describe the behavior of human packs. In the prayers and readings of Holy Week the psalms in which persecutors are cursed play a major role. The liturgy requires us to reread the complaints of these narrators who are about to be lynched, and it does this to help us better understand the sufferings of Christ, while showing us more ordinary human beings grappling with similar injustice. This injustice is no doubt less than what Jesus suffered, for he is totally devoted to those who persecute him, but the psalm narrators relate human experiences that are close to Jesus' sufferings in the Passion.

Modern exegetes don't see the relevance of the close connection between the psalms and the Passion because they don't understand crowd phenomena in all their violent absurdity. Not perceiving the real violence in the psalms, they don't understand that the psalm narrators and Jesus are really victims of the same type of injustice. The biblical texts that demystify incidents of contagious escalation and the mimetic war of all against one actually "announce" or "pre-figure" the sufferings of Christ. We cannot sympathize with these victims without sympathizing equally with Jesus, and vice versa: we cannot despise the sufferings of persons who appear to be the most insignificant, the beggar of Ephesus, for example, without spiritually joining the persecutors of Jesus.

We find here the essence of specifically Judeo-Christian prophetic religion. It is closely related to the suffering that all collective persecutions produce, whatever their date in human history, whatever the ethnic, religious, or cultural attributes of the victims. The modern scorn for the notion of the prophetic, the idea that prophecy is a theological mirage outdated by a "scientific method" that is necessarily superior to the texts and ideas it studies, is a more terrible superstition than ancient credulity, for its arrogance makes it completely closed to any comprehension. False science is blind to mimetic cycles in general and the way in which the Bible progressively reveals them from one end to the other. This revelation justifies the idea of Old Testament "prefiguration" and christological "fulfillment."

The Jewish prophets had already proceeded in the same way as the Gospels. To combat the blindness of the crowds and to defend themselves against the hatred directed against their pessimistic insight and discernment, they resorted to examples of incomprehension and persecution of which earlier prophets were the victims. Traditional Christian liturgy draws liberally from these texts whose sensitivity to collective injustice is extremely strong, whereas in philosophical texts it is very weak and in mythical texts it is null. Seeing as "prophetic" the interrelation of all the texts that denounce persecutory illusions is based on a profound intuition of the continuity between the Hebrew Bible and the Gospels. This idea has nothing to do with what passes as prophetic in popular perception: fantastic claims to divination that are common in most societies.

When we read a great Christian thinker like Pascal, we find, regretfully, that he conceives prophecy as a kind of mechanical code, a sort of puzzle that only Christians are able to solve because they have the key to it. The Jews, on the other hand, are accounted as understanding nothing about their own texts because they don't possess this key, which is the very person of Christ. But with the mimetic interpretation it is possible to construe the idea of prophecy in a positive sense just as much for the Jews as for the Christians. This positive sense excludes no one, certainly not the writers of the oldest texts who were prophetically inspired. We can see this in their defense of the innocence of a victim unjustly condemned. To understand prophecy we must trace it back, like everything that is essential in Christianity, to charity, to concern for the poor, the

weak, the disinherited, the lowly. We must see its place in the parable in Matthew about the final judgment: "Truly I say to you, in as
much as you have done [deeds of charity and mercy] to one of the
least of these my brothers, you have done it unto me" (25:40).

The Christian revelation in its highest sense is always aware of
the biblical revelation that precedes it. It is basically of the same
nature and proceeds from the same type of insight. The Christian
revelation in its highest sense desires to be guided on the basis of the
older, related revelation, to be enriched by its treasury of knowledge
and its marvelously concrete and picturesque forms of speech. The
Old Testament quotations that the Gospel writers strew through
their narratives don't seem all equally relevant. Occasionally they
seem particularly verbal, devoid of profound meaning, generating
artificial correspondences with the Hebrew Bible. But it's a bad idea
to condemn Holy Scripture hastily. When we feel like dismissing
Scripture, we should watch out. Perhaps we are not, at that moment,
up to what our task requires.

The Gospel revelation is the definitive formulation of a truth
already partially disclosed in the Old Testament. But in order to
come to completion, it requires the good news that God himself
accepts the role of the victim of the crowd so that he can save us
all. This God who becomes a victim is not another mythic god but
the one God, infinitely good, of the Old Testament.

The divinization of Christ is not based on the illusion of mimetic
snowballing, which produces the sacred of myth. To the contrary,
it is based on the full and complete revelation of the truth that
demystifies mythology, and it is this truth, I hope, that nourishes my
own analyses from the beginning. Against the mythic deities stands
a God who does not emerge from the misunderstanding regarding
victims but who voluntarily assumes the role of the single victim
and makes possible, for the first time, the full disclosure of the single
victim mechanism.

This is not to regress toward mythology. On the contrary, Christianity represents a new stage of the biblical revelation beyond the

Old Testament. Far from relapsing into the divinization of victims and the victimization of the divine that characterizes mythology, as many people inevitably imagine, the divinity of Jesus obliges us to distinguish two types of transcendence externally similar but radically opposed. The one type is false, deceptive, misleading, and it is the unconscious fulfillment of the victim mechanism. The other transcendence is truthful, luminous, and it destroys mythical illusions by revealing how violent contagion poisons communities. It reveals how poison is used to counteract poison, a "remedy" to evil whose source is the evil itself. This second transcendence is the true one that begins in the Old Testament and comes to full bloom in the New Testament.

The divinity of Christ is fully revealed when he is the victim of the mimetic event of all against one, but it owes absolutely nothing to this phenomenon of violent contagion and scapegoating. To the contrary, he subverts it.

To STRENGTHEN the preceding argument, I would like now to comment on two passages in the synoptic Gospels that show not only the deceptive resemblances between the false and the true manifestations of the divine but something even more remarkable: the existence of an evangelical or Gospel knowledge regarding these resemblances and the misunderstandings they entail. For the Gospel writers, assimilating the divinity of Christ to a mythic divinization is so impossible that they can present events likely to reinforce this sort of confusion without the least embarrassment or anxiety. If they were nothing but vulgar propagandists, as so many of our experts suspect, then Matthew, Mark, and Luke would never have written the two accounts that I will now discuss.

THE FIRST PASSAGE, quite brief, is in the Gospel of Luke. I have already said that the death of Jesus appeases the multitude. It produces the same effect on the crowd as all collective murders or murders inspired by a crowd, a kind of relaxation of tension, a sacrificial *catharsis* that prevents the riot Pilate fears. From the standpoint of the Gospels and Christianity this appeasement of the crowd has, of course, no religious value. It is a phenomenon typical of violent contagion, of human beings who are prisoners of Satan.

Instead of confusing and mystifying the process of the victim mechanism, the Gospels demystify it by exposing the purely mimetic nature of what a mythic account would take for divine. The Gospel of Luke contains proof of this, a brief but very revealing indication of demystification. It's a precious bit of evidence for the alert interpreter. At the end of his account of the Passion Luke adds this observation: "And that same day Herod and Pilate became friends, for before this they had been enemies" (23:12). According to the Gospel of Luke Jesus appeared briefly before Herod. And it is their common participation in the death of Jesus that brings Herod and Pilate together. Their reconciliation is one of those cathartic effects that benefit the participants in a collective murder, the unrepentant persecutors. It is the most characteristic effect of these murders. If it is powerful enough, it leads to the mythic deification of the victim.

Luke clearly perceives this effect. He well understands that the improvement of relations between Herod and Pilate has nothing Christian about it. Why then does he go to the trouble of pointing out a detail lacking any Christian value? It's highly unlikely he is interested in "Palestinian politics." What does interest him, evidently, is what I am talking about here, the pacifying effect of collective murder. But why is he, a Christian, interested in this typically pagan reconciliation of the two statesmen?

I think Luke points out this reconciliation so that we may recognize something that, viewed from the outside, resembles the effect of the sacrament of the Eucharist among the first Christians and could be confused with it. He certainly does not confuse the reconciliation of the two representatives of the principalities and powers with what will happen between the disciples and Jesus when the Resurrection occurs. It is the *paradox of the resemblance* between mythical and Christian reconciliation that strikes Luke, and he does not hesitate to report this and does not fear there will be any confusion. That he brings the two resurrections, the true and the false, into contact with one another is a matter of great interest in an intellectual as well as a spiritual sense.

If we are really faithful to the Gospels, *we* will not suppress what makes the Passion a single victim mechanism similar to all others. Our taking this mechanism carefully into account does not endanger the Christian theological interpretation of the Cross but strengthens it. The facts and patterns on which mythic deifications are based are all present in the Passion stories, but they are not misunderstood, nor do they go unrecognized as they would in a myth. Rather they are understood, demystified, neutralized.

Pilate and Herod don't realize, most probably, that their becoming friends again stems from the death of Jesus. Luke possesses the awareness that they lack. Of the four Gospel writers, he is the one who best defines the collective reality of the persecutory unconscious.

Now LET US TURN to the second passage that I wish to discuss, the oldest of the two according to most New Testament scholars because it is found in the Gospels of Mark and Matthew. It is longer than the first one. It is the account of Herod's false belief in the resurrection of his victim, John the Baptist. This text is a marvelous illustration of the problem of the striking, startling resemblances between mythical resurrections and the resurrection of Jesus.

Now Mark and Matthew, as Christian writers, clearly hold that Herod's belief in John's resurrection is false whereas Jesus' resurrection is true. What makes this text so extraordinary is that the actual death of John and his false resurrection look from the outside like the actual death and real resurrection of Jesus. From the outside they seem so much alike that this text in the Gospels is nothing short of amazing for modern readers, whether they are Christian or not.

The two beliefs, one true and the other false, both have their roots in one or another of those collective murders, or collectively inspired murders, out of which the mythic gods emerge. In both cases the adherents affirm the resurrection of a venerated prophet.

In both cases the resurrection appears to spring out of collective violence.

The two Gospels put into Herod's mouth a sentence that clearly suggests the origin of his false belief in his obsessive recollection of the murder: "The one I beheaded, this John, he has been raised up!" (Mark 6:16). This sentence situates the false resurrection in direct continuity with the violent death, which thus appears to be a founding death. It confirms the conception of mythic origins I have proposed in preceding chapters. The entire episode is a mythic origin story in miniature, strangely similar to the sequence of the Passion and the Resurrection.

Immediately after Herod's statement the two Gospels go back in time to recount the murder of John. What justifies the account of the murder can only be the concern to explain Herod's false belief. To give an account of a false resurrection, it is necessary to recognize the collective murder that gives rise to it. How otherwise would one justify the going back in time of the narrative in the two Gospels, which use the technique of the "flashback"? There is no other example of this in the Gospels.

Matthew even more than Mark underscores the generative function of the murder in Herod's belief. For Mark the belief in John's resurrection begins, not with Herod himself, but with the popular rumors that Herod believed, and of course Herod had been fascinated with John ("When he heard him he was greatly perplexed; and yet he heard him gladly"). But Matthew doesn't mention the rumors. In his Gospel the false belief in the prophet's resurrection has no other cause than Herod's participation in John's murder.

Matthew and Mark don't say anything to clear up the disarray into which the two resurrections, the false and the true, threatens to plunge so many timid Christians impressed by modern skepticism. The Gospel writers obviously do not share the doubts that the resemblance of the two accounts may create for our contemporaries. If these similarities had troubled them, they would have done what Luke did, which is to suppress this episode. It is an episode not centered on Jesus and so plays a secondary role. It could have been easily eliminated. Mark and Matthew have a faith too strong and pure to get worried, as we do nowadays, over similarities between the false resurrection and the true one. It seems that the two writers emphasize these resemblances in order to show the points where the satanic imitations of the truth are most impressive and yet ineffectual.

Christian faith consists in this: to think and believe that the resurrection of Christ owes nothing to human violence, by contrast to mythic resurrections, which really stem from collective murders. The resurrection of Christ comes about after his death, inevitably but not immediately; it happens only on the third day, and if we look through a Christian lens, it has its origin in God himself.

What separates the true resurrection from the false are not thematic differences in the drama preceding it, since all this is very similar. The difference lies in the power of revelation. We have already confirmed this power, and we will confirm it again in the chapters to come. It opposes so decisively the power of the mythic cover-up that once we perceive this opposition, the thematic resemblances between myth and Gospel fade into insignificance by comparison. Everything that haunts so-called scientific criticism, everything that seems to confirm the skepticism that critics bring with them before beginning their work, comes across as self-fulfilling prophecy, a vicious circle of mimetic illusion.

The Gospels always "verify," in a marvelous way, all the positions that we adopt regarding them, even those contradicting their true spirit. We can detect a "superior" irony in these verifications, brilliant in appearance yet illusory, that the Gospels provide for their "scientific" readers.

Luke suppressed the account of the murder of John the Baptist, I believe, because he saw in it a regrettable digression, not because he was troubled by it. His intention was to make Jesus the sole center of his narrative.

It could be that in Luke's Gospel the brief mention of the reconciliation of Herod and Pilate is what corresponds to the false resurrection in Matthew and Mark. Belief in the false resurrection is a pagan touch characteristic of representatives of the "powers" such as Herod. Luke suppresses it, but he replaces it with another pagan touch of the same type, the reconciliation of Herod and Pilate as a result of the Crucifixion. What the Gospels suggest and reject in both cases is the process of mythic deification.

In spite of appearances, the Gospels and their proclamation of the resurrection of Jesus stand in opposition to mythology even more radically than the Old Testament. We see the Gospels giving proof of a knowledge that is dizzying. They dare to draw our attention to the uncanny similarities between the false and the true resurrections, because they never doubt for one second the spuriousness of the one and the reality of the other. Unbelievers, by contrast, confuse the two.

Chapter 11

The Triumph of the Cross

F ROM AN ANTHROPOLOGICAL STANDPOINT I would define Christian revelation as the true *representation*[1] of what had never been
completely represented or what had been falsely represented: the
mimetic convergence of all against one, the single victim mechanism with its antecedent developments, particularly "interdividual"[2]
scandals.

Mythology falsifies this mechanism to the detriment of victims
and to the advantage of persecutors of the victim. The Hebrew Bible
frequently suggests the truth, evokes it, and even partially represents
it, but never completely and perfectly. The Gospels, taken in their
totality, *are* this representation, precisely and perfectly.

Once we understand this, a passage from the letter to the
Colossians, which appears obscure at first, becomes illuminating:

[Christ has] canceled the accusation that stands against us with
its legal claims. He set it aside, nailing it to the cross. He thus disarmed the principalities and powers and made a public spectacle
of them, drawing them along in his triumph. (Col. 2:14–15)

---

1. "Representation" is a key notion in this chapter. Girard is talking about representation as
presenting some subject or event *again*, but not simply in the form of primitive ritual, which is
initially a reflexive imitation that is blind and unaware of itself. Representation requires some
reflection on what is represented and extensive development. In an interview I conducted for
The Girard Reader Girard says, "It may have taken hundreds of thousands of years, or longer, to
reach the representational capacity of 'humanity'" (New York: Crossroad, 1996), 269. — Trans.

2. "Interdividual" is a neologism Girard has used, particularly in *Things Hidden since the Foundation of the World*, trans. S. Bann and M. Metteer (Stanford: Stanford University Press, 1987),
to emphasize that human beings are never autonomous "individuals." We are constituted by the
other, that is, by parents, authority figures, peers, rivals whom we internalize as models and who
become the unconscious basis of our desires. This does not mean that freedom of the will is not
possible. Humankind as created in the image of God is not intended to be *identical* to the other
or exist in *slavish subservience* to the other. However, since we learn first and primarily through
mimesis, our freedom depends on being constituted by the other. — Trans.

The accusation against humankind is the accusation against the innocent victim that we find in the myths. To hold the principalities and powers responsible for it is the same thing as holding Satan himself responsible, in his role of *public prosecutor* that I have already mentioned.

Before Christ and the Bible the satanic accusation was always victorious by virtue of the violent contagion that imprisoned human beings within systems of myth and ritual. The Crucifixion reduces mythology to powerlessness by exposing violent contagion, which is so effective in the myths that it prevents communities from ever finding out the truth, namely, the innocence of their victims.

This accusation temporarily relieves communities of their violence, but it turns back again and "stands against" the persecutors, for it subjects them to Satan, or in other words to the principalities and powers with their deceitful gods and bloody sacrifices. Jesus, in showing his innocence in the Passion accounts, has "canceled" this accusation; he "set it aside." He nails the accusation to the Cross, which is to say that he reveals its falsity. Though ordinarily the accusation nails the victim to a cross, here by contrast the accusation itself is nailed and publicly exhibited and exposed as a lie. The Cross enables the truth to triumph because the Gospels disclose the falseness of the accusation; they unmask Satan as an imposter. Or to say it in another way, they discredit once and for all the untruth of the principalities and powers in the wake of the Cross. The Cross of Christ restores all the victims of the single victim mechanism, whether it goes under the label of legal accusation, Satan, or principalities and powers.

As Satan was making humans obligated to him, putting them in his debt, he was making them accomplices in his crimes. The Cross, by revealing the lie at the bottom of Satan's game, exposes human beings to a temporary increase of violence, but at a deeper level it liberates them from a servitude that has lasted since the beginning of human history, since "the foundation of the world."

It is not only the accusation that Christ has nailed to the Cross and publicly exhibited; the principalities and powers themselves are paraded, in full public view, in the triumphal process of the crucified Christ, so in a way they too are crucified. These metaphors are not at all fantastic and badly improvised; they are so precise it takes your breath away. Why? Because the revealer and what is revealed are one: the mimetic war of all against one, concealed in Satan and the powers, is revealed in the crucifixion of Christ as narrated in the truthful accounts of his Passion.

The Cross and the satanic origin of the false religions and the powers are one and the same phenomenon, revealed in one case, concealed in the other. This is why Dante, in his *Inferno*, represented Satan as nailed to the Cross.[3] When the single victim mechanism is correctly nailed to the Cross, its ultimately banal, insignificant basis appears in broad daylight, and everything based on it gradually loses its prestige, grows more and more feeble, and finally disappears.

The principal metaphor is *triumph in the Roman* sense, which is the reward that Rome bestowed on its victorious generals. Standing on his chariot, the victorious general made a solemn entrance into the city and received the acclamations of the crowd. The enemy leaders, in chains, were led along at the rear of the procession. Before the Romans executed these prisoners, they exhibited them like ferocious beasts reduced to utter helplessness. Vercingetorix played this role in the triumph of Caesar. The victorious general here is Christ, and his victory is the Cross. What Christianity conquers is the pagan way of organizing the world. The enemy leaders in chains behind their conqueror are the principalities and powers. The author compares the irresistible power of the Cross to the power of military might, the Roman army, which was still utterly dominant when he wrote.

Of all the Christian ideas, none nowadays arouses more sarcasm than the one that our text expresses so openly, the idea of a *triumph of the Cross*. To progressive Christians, proud of their humility, it seems as arrogant as it is absurd. To characterize the attitude that they condemn, they have brought the term "triumphalism"

---

3. See John Freccero, *The Poetics of Conversion* (Cambridge, Mass.: Harvard University Press, 1986): "The Sign of Satan," 167–79.

into fashion. If there exists somewhere a charter of triumphalism, it must be the text I am discussing here. It may seem to be expressly written to arouse the indignation of modernists, who are always very concerned to summon the Church to its obligation of humility.

But this metaphor of triumph contains a paradox so evident that it has to be deliberate, and it must stem from irony. Military violence is as alien as possible to the intention of the letter to the Colossians. The victory of Christ has nothing to do with the military triumph of a victorious general: rather than inflicting violence on others, Christ submits to it. What we should retain in the image of triumph is not the military aspect but the idea of an extraordinary event offered to the view of all humankind, a public exhibition of what the enemy had to conceal in order to defend himself. The Cross has stripped away this defense, this reality that exists through deception.

Christ does not achieve this victory through violence. He obtains it through a renunciation of violence so complete that violence can rage to its heart's content without realizing that by so doing, it reveals what it must conceal, without suspecting that its fury will turn back against it this time because it will be recorded and represented with exactness in the Passion narratives.

If we do not detect the role of mimetic contagion in the genesis of social orders, the idea that the principalities and powers are disarmed and exposed by the Cross will appear absurd, a pure and simple inversion of the truth. But our text affirms that the Crucifixion produces just the contrary of this standard wisdom. This wisdom says that the principalities and powers nailed Christ to the Cross and stripped him of everything without any damage at all to themselves, without endangering themselves. Our text thus boldly contradicts everything so-called common sense regards as the hard and sad truth about the Passion. The powers are not invisible; they are dazzling presences in our world. They hold the first rank. They never stop strutting and flaunting their power and riches. There's no need to make an exhibition of them: they put themselves on permanent exhibition.

The idea of the triumph of the Cross seems so absurd in the

eyes of the so-called scientific exegetes that they readily see it as one of those complete inversions that desperate people force on the real world when their own world founders and they can no longer face the truth. This is what psychiatrists call "compensation." People devastated by a completely overwhelming catastrophe, without any concrete hope, reverse all the signs that inform them about the real world. They make a "plus" out of every "minus" and a "minus" out of every "plus," which is exactly what happened to the disciples of Jesus after the Crucifixion—the believers call it the Resurrection, but wise skepticism scoffs at such nonsense.

This sociological-psychological approach is the real nonsense. The precision and sobriety of the accounts of the Crucifixion, also their unity, more pronounced than the rest of the Gospels, in no way give the impression of reflecting the kind of psychic catastrophe and despair, of rupture with reality, that the critics imagine.

It is possible to give a good and rational explanation of the triumph of the Cross without recourse to psychological hypotheses. The triumph of the Cross reflects and corresponds to a tangible reality that can be rationally apprehended. The Cross has indeed transformed the world, and we can interpret its power in a way that does not have to appeal to religious faith. We can give the triumph of the Cross a plausible meaning in a completely rational frame of reference. When they reflect on the Cross, most people see only the brutality of the event. The terrible death of Jesus takes place, it seems, in a manner that gives the lie to "triumphalism" in the most decisive fashion. However, beside the event in all its brutality, which works to the advantage of the principalities and powers since it rids them of Jesus, there is another history that goes unrecognized by most historians and yet is just as objective as the stuff we find in textbooks. This is the history, not of the events themselves, but of their *representation*.

Behind the myths there is an event that governs them, but the myths do not allow us to identify it, for they distort it and transform it. But to repeat what I have already insisted on, the Gospels *represent* this event as it is, in all its reality, and they make this reality, this truth, which human societies had never identified, available to all humanity.

Outside of the Passion accounts and the songs of the Servant of Yahweh, the principalities and powers are visible in their external splendor, but they are invisible and unknown in their interior, in their shameful, violent origin. The reality behind the scenes is nowhere available except in a few Old Testament texts and the Passion narratives. For everything pertaining to their false glory, the powers don't hesitate to take charge of their own publicity. But the Cross reveals their violent origin, which must remain concealed to prevent their collapse. This is what our text expresses in the image of the principalities and powers as a "public spectacle" as they bring up the rear of the procession that Christ leads in victory.

By nailing Christ to the Cross, the powers believed they were doing what they ordinarily did in unleashing the single victim mechanism. They thought they were avoiding the danger of disclosure. They did not suspect that in the end they would be doing just the opposite: they would be contributing to their own annihilation, nailing themselves to the Cross, so to speak. They did not and could not suspect the revelatory power of the Cross.

By depriving the victim mechanism of the darkness that must conceal it so it can continue to control human culture, the Cross shakes up the world. Its light deprives Satan of his principal power, the power to expel Satan. Once the Cross completely illuminates this dark sun, Satan is no longer able to limit his capacity for destruction. Satan will destroy his kingdom, and he will destroy himself.

To understand this is to understand why Paul sees the Cross as the source of all knowledge about the world and human beings as well as about God. When Paul asserts that he wants to know nothing besides Christ crucified, he is not engaging in "anti-intellectualism." He is not announcing his contempt for knowledge. Paul believes quite literally that there is no knowledge superior to knowing the crucified Christ. If we go to this school, we will learn more about God and humankind simultaneously than if we look to any other source of knowledge. His suffering on the Cross is the price Jesus is willing to pay in order to offer humanity this true representation of human origins that holds it prisoner. In offering himself in this way, he deprives the victim mechanism of its power in the long run.

In the triumph of a victorious general the humiliating display of those who are conquered is only a consequence of the victory achieved, whereas in the case of the Cross this display is the victory itself; it is the unveiling of the violent origin of culture. The powers are not put on display because they are defeated, but they are defeated because they are put on display.

There is an irony, therefore, in the metaphor of military triumph, and what gives it its edge is the fact that Satan and his cohorts respect nothing but power. They think only in terms of military triumph. They are beaten by a weapon whose effectiveness they could not conceive, that contradicts all their beliefs, all their values. It is the most radical weakness that defeats the power of satanic self-expulsion.

To UNDERSTAND the difference between mythology and the Gospels, between mythic concealment and Christian revelation, we must avoid confusing the representation with what is represented.

Many readers imagine that when something is represented in a text, then the text is under the sway of its own representation. They think that the single victim mechanism must dominate the Gospels because only in them, and nowhere else, is it really visible. By the same token, they take this same mechanism as absent from mythology because the myths never represent it, because they give no explicit indication of its presence.

These exegetes are astonished then to hear me say that collective murder is essential to the generation of myths, and that it has nothing to do with the origin of the Gospels. The Gospels *present it again* or *re-present it,* but their origin lies in the life and deeds and teachings of Christ, whose love and suffering reveal our violence for what it is. Collective murder, or the single victim mechanism, has everything to do with the origin of the texts that do not represent it and cannot represent it precisely because they are based on it, because the victim mechanism is their generating principle. These texts are the myths.

The exegetes are dupes of the modern bias of concluding too quickly that texts dealing with collective violence are violent texts whose violence we have the duty to denounce. Under the influence of the Nietzsche tradition (see chapter 14), our bias tends to function on the principle of "no smoke without fire." This is as mystifying as can be in the subject concerning us here. The exegetes treat the Judeo-Christian revelation as a kind of Freudian or Nietzschean symptom in the sense of the "slave morality." They see the revelation of the victim mechanism as the leveling effect of social resentment, for example. They never wonder whether by chance this revelation may be justified.

Only wherever it is *not* represented can mimetic snowballing play a generative role due to the very fact that it is not represented, that it misunderstands itself. As soon as mimetic contagion has taken over the community, its members are possessed by it. Violent contagion speaks for them; mimetic violence pronounces the guilt of the victim and the innocence of the persecutors. The community no longer speaks; the speaker is rather the one the Gospels name as the *accuser*, Satan.

Pseudoscientific exegetes don't see that the biblical basis of Judaism and Christianity transmits the first revelatory and liberating representations regarding violence. Violence has always existed, but until the biblical revelation it remained concealed in the infrastructure of mythology. Under the influence of Nietzsche and Freud, our contemporaries go and find in these texts, whose referentiality is denied without the least proof, various indications of a "persecution complex" with which Judaism and Christianity as a whole are alleged to be afflicted. Mythology, on the other hand, is held to be exempt from this complex.

The proof that all this is absurd is the superb indifference, the regal contempt, that mythology shows toward any suggestion of possible violence of the strong against the weak, of those in the majority against the minority, of the healthy against the ill, of the normal against the abnormal, of the native against the foreigners, and so on.

Modern confidence in the myths is even stranger in our day when our contemporaries are terribly suspicious regarding their own society. They see hidden victims everywhere except where they really are, in the myths that they never look at with a critical eye.

Contemporary thinkers, still under Nietzschean influence, have the habit of seeing the myths as kindly texts, sympathetic, cheerful, and lively. Mythology is regarded as superior in every way to the Jewish and Christian Scriptures, which are dominated, not by a legitimate concern for justice and truth, but by morbid suspicion. Most intellectuals in the present world seem to adopt this perspective. What sells this view is the apparent absence of unjust violence in the myths or the aesthetic transformation of violent deeds. By contrast, the Jewish and Christian Scriptures come across as so obsessed with persecutions that their relationship to them must at least suggest their own guilt. To grasp this misunderstanding in its enormity, we must see it in light of a case of unjust condemnation of a victim. My example is the famous Dreyfus case, an affair so thoroughly clarified that it now eliminates any possibility of misunderstanding.

In the late nineteenth and early twentieth centuries, when Captain Dreyfus, condemned for a crime he had not committed, was serving his sentence, there were, on one side, the "anti-Dreyfus" people, who were numerous and perfectly serene and satisfied, for they had their collective victim, and they congratulated themselves on seeing him justly punished. On the other side were the defenders of Dreyfus, very, very few at first. For a long time people viewed them as obvious traitors or professional malcontents, always occupied with chewing over all sorts of grievances and suspicions whose real basis no one around them could see. Critics looked for the motives of their behavior in personal morbidity or political prejudices.

In fact, anti-Dreyfusism was a true myth, a false accusation that the accusers confused with truth. Mimetic contagion maintained a contagion so kindled by anti-Semitic prejudice that no disclosure of the real facts of the case during these years succeeded in shaking it.

Those who celebrate the "innocence" of the myths, their joy in life, and their healthy outlook and who put all that in opposition to the sickly suspicion of the Hebrew Bible and the Gospels commit a grave error. It is the same error, in my view, as those who opted for anti-Dreyfusism against Dreyfusism. One writer and poet of that period, Charles Péguy (1873–1914), perceived the analogy with the Passion of Christ.

If the supporters of Dreyfus had not fought for their point of view, if they had not suffered (at least some of them) for the truth, if they had admitted, as have some in our day, that to believe there is such a thing as truth is the fundamental sin—then Dreyfus would never have been vindicated, and the lie would have won the victory.

If we admire the myths that don't detect the innocent victims in their own stories and condemn the Bible because it does, then we relapse into the illusion of the anti-Dreyfus majority, which refused to consider the possibility of a judicial error. Through much struggle and suffering the supporters of Dreyfus achieved a triumph for a truth as absolute, intransigent, and dogmatic as Joseph's in his opposition to mythological violence.

THE VICTIM MECHANISM is not a literary theme like many others; it is a principle of illusion. As such, it cannot appear at all in the texts it controls. If this mechanism appears explicitly as a principle of illusion, as it does in the Old Testament and New Testament, it does not dominate them in the sense that it dominates texts where it remains invisible, unsuspected, as in the myths.

No text can illuminate the process of mimetic snowballing on which it is based; no text can have its basis in the violent contagion it illuminates. Thus we must guard against confusing the question of the victim of the unanimous crowd with what the literary critic talks about, namely, a *theme* or *motif* that we ascribe to a writer when it shows up in his or her writings, and that we don't ascribe, of course, if it does not show up.

It is easy to recognize this error, but it is even easier not to recognize it, and as a rule, it goes unrecognized. Hardly anyone suspects that if the myths never speak of arbitrary violence, this could be because they unknowingly reflect the virulence of a persecution that does not recognize its victims anywhere but sees them as justly expelled culprits—victims like Oedipus, for example, who are supposed to have "really" committed parricide and incest.

It is mimetic contagion that completely determines the contents of mythology. The myths are so much in its thrall that they cannot suspect their own subjection. No text can make allusion to the principle of illusion that governs it.

To be a victim of illusion is to take it for true, so it means one is unable to express it as such, as illusion. By being the first to point out persecutory illusion, the Bible initiates a revolution that, through Christianity, spreads little by little to all humanity without being really understood by those whose profession and pride are to understand everything. This is one of the reasons, I believe, Jesus speaks the literal truth when he exclaims: "I thank you, Father ... that you have hidden these things from the wise and clever and revealed them to babes" (Matt. 11:25).

The necessary condition enabling the single victim mechanism to dominate a text is that it does not appear as an explicit theme. And vice versa: a victim mechanism cannot dominate a text—the Gospels—in which it explicitly appears. This involves a paradox that forces us to see our dreadful blindness to the greatness of the Passion accounts. It is always the individual or the revelatory text that is taken to be responsible for the inexcusable violence it reveals. We tend, in short, to hold the messenger responsible for the unpleasantness of the message, as Cleopatra does in Shakespeare's play. The specific character of myths is to hide their own violence. It is the character of the Jewish and Christian Scriptures to reveal the same violence and to suffer the consequences in the eyes of blind humanity.

The principle of illusion or victim mechanism cannot appear in broad daylight without losing its structuring power. In order to be effective, it demands the ignorance of persecutors who "do not know what they are doing." It demands the darkness of Satan to function adequately.

The myths are not aware of their own violence, which they project upon the higher transcendent level by demonizing and then deifying their victims. It is just this transfigured violence that becomes visible in the Bible. The victims are seen as true victims, no longer guilty but innocent. The persecutors are seen as true persecutors, no longer innocent but guilty. It is not merely our predecessors whom we unceasingly accuse who are guilty; we all stand in need of pardon.

A myth is a lie in the sense that it is the deceptive nonrepresentation that mimetic contagion and its victim mechanism generate by means of the community that becomes their instrument. The mimetic contagion is never objectified; it is never represented in the mythic narrative. It is its *real* subject, therefore, but it is always concealed as such. It is what the Gospels call Satan, or the devil.

THE PROOF that it is difficult, or perhaps too easy, to understand what I have just said is that Satan himself did not understand it. Or rather, he understood it, but too late to protect his realm. His slowness has had tremendous consequences for human history.

Paul writes to the Corinthians: "If the princes of this world had known [the wisdom of God] they would not have crucified the Lord of glory" (1 Cor. 2:8). "The princes of this world" are here the same thing as Satan; they crucified the Lord of glory because they expected the results of this event to be favorable to their interests. They were hoping that the victim mechanism would function as usual, protected from any suspicions, and that they would thus rid themselves of Jesus and his message. At the beginning of the matter they had very good reason to think that everything would happen cleanly and quickly.

The crucifixion of Jesus is a victim mechanism like the others; it is set in motion and develops like the others. Yet its outcome is different from all the others.

Until the Resurrection no one could foresee the reversal of the violent contagion that almost completely overcame the disciples themselves. The princes of this world could rub their hands in satisfaction, and yet it turned out that their calculations were undone. Instead of conjuring away once more the secret of the single victim mechanism, the four accounts of the Passion broadcast it to the four corners of the world, publicizing it wherever they were read and proclaimed.

Starting from Paul's statement that I have just quoted, Origen and many of the Greek Fathers elaborated a thesis that played a great role as the first centuries of Christianity unfolded, that of *Satan duped by the Cross*.[4] Satan means the same in this formulation as those St. Paul names as the "princes of this world." In Western Christianity this thesis has not met with the same favor as in the East, and finally, as far as I know, it disappeared. Western theologians suspected it of being "magical thought." They have wondered whether it attributes a role to God that is unworthy.

The thesis interprets the Cross as a kind of divine trap, a ruse of God that is even stronger and cleverer than Satan's ruses. Certain Fathers amplified this idea into a strange metaphor that contributed to the distrust in the West. Christ is compared to the bait the fisher puts on the hook to catch a hungry fish, and that fish is Satan.

The role this discourse ascribes to Satan troubles the Western thinkers. As times passes, the devil's place shrinks in Western theological thought. His disappearance is troublesome to the extent that Satan is the same thing as mimetic contagion, which alone can clarify the true meaning and validity of the patristic metaphor of Satan duped by the Cross. The discovery of the mimetic, or satanic, cycle enables us to understand that this metaphor contains an essential insight. It takes into account the fact that mimetic conflicts and mimetic pride are the main obstacle to the Christian revelation.

Mythical-ritual societies are prisoners of a mimetic circle that they cannot escape since they are unable to identify it. This continues

---

4. Jean Daniélou, *Origène* (Paris: La table ronde, 1948), 264–69.

to be true today: all our ideas about humankind, all our philoso-
phies, all our social sciences, all our psychological theories, etc.
are fundamentally pagan because they are based on a blindness to
the circularity of mimetic conflict and contagion. This blindness is
similar to that of mythical-ritual systems.

The Passion accounts, allowing us to understand the single victim mechanism and its mimetic cycles, enable us to find and identify
our invisible prison and to comprehend our need for redemption.
Since the "princes of this world" were not in communion with
God, they did not understand that the victim mechanism they un-
leashed against Jesus would result in truthful accounts. If they had
been able to read the future, not only would they not have en-
couraged the Crucifixion, but they would have opposed it with all
their might.

When the princes of this world finally understood the real import
of the Cross, it was too late to turn back: Jesus had been crucified,
and the Gospels had been written. Thus Paul is right to affirm: "If
the princes of this world had known [the wisdom of God] they would
not have crucified the Lord of glory." Western theology, in rejecting
the idea of Satan tricked by the Cross, has lost a pearl of great price
in the sphere of anthropology.

Medieval and modern theories of redemption all look in the direction of God for the causes of the Crucifixion: God's honor, God's
justice, even God's anger, must be satisfied. These theories don't
succeed because they don't seriously look in the direction where the
answer must lie: sinful humanity, human relations, mimetic contagion, which is the same thing as Satan. They speak much of original
sin, but they fail to make the idea concrete. That is why they give
an impression of being arbitrary and unjust to human beings, even
if they are theologically sound.

Once we identify the bad contagion, the idea of Satan duped
by the Cross acquires a precise meaning that the Greeks obviously
sensed without succeeding in articulating it in a completely satisfying fashion. To be a "child of the devil" in the sense of the Gospel of
John, as we have seen, is to be locked into a deceptive system of mi-

metic contagion that can only lead into systems of myth and ritual. Or, in our time, it leads into those more recent forms of idolatry, such as ideology or the cult of science.

The Greek Fathers had it right in saying that with the Cross Satan is the mystifier caught in the trap of his own mystification. The single victim mechanism was his personal property, his very own thing, the instrument of self-expulsion that put the world at his feet. But in the Cross this mechanism escapes once and for all from the control Satan exercised over it, and as a result the world looks completely different.

If God allowed Satan to reign for a certain period over humankind, it is because God knew beforehand that at the right time Christ would overcome his adversary by dying on the Cross. God in his wisdom had foreseen since the beginning that the victim mechanism would be reversed like a glove, exposed, placed in the open, stripped naked, and dismantled in the Gospel Passion texts, and he knew that neither Satan nor the powers could prevent this revelation.

In triggering the victim mechanism against Jesus, Satan believed he was protecting his kingdom, defending his possession, not realizing that, in fact, he was doing the very opposite. He did exactly what God had foreseen. Only Satan could have set in motion the process of his own destruction without suspecting anything was wrong.

All we need to make the thesis of Satan duped by the Cross intelligible is a clear definition of what imprisons human beings in the realm of Satan: mimetic contagion and its outcome in the victim mechanism have provided us with that definition. We should not conclude that to identify the truth is enough to liberate us from the lies in which we are all imprisoned.

The apostle Paul's text, from which I took the sentence that I just commented on, is the expression of extraordinary inspiration. Paul there intuits the existence of a divine plan that bears on all of human history, but he cannot quite formulate it. He goes into what may almost be called "ecstatic stammering" for lack of a language that could perform the task. He evokes a secret and hidden wisdom of God, which God decreed before the ages for our glory. None of the rulers of this age understood this, for if they had known they would not have crucified the Lord of glory. But as it is written, "What eye has not seen, nor ear heard, nor the heart of man conceived, God has prepared for those who love him." (1 Cor. 2:7–9)

God permitted Satan to reign for a time over humanity, foreseeing that at the appointed time God would overcome him on the Cross. The divine wisdom knew that thanks to this death the victim mechanism would be neutralized. Satan would be completely unable to elude this trap; he would participate in God's plan unawares. The Greek Fathers, in treating Satan as the victim of a kind of divine ruse, suggest aspects of revelation now obscured because the anthropology of the Cross remains obscure.

Satan himself has thus placed the truth at the disposal of humankind; he has made it possible to overturn his own lie; he has rendered the truth of God universally understandable.

The idea of Satan duped by the Cross is therefore not magical at all and in no way offends the dignity of God. The trick that traps Satan does not include the least bit of either violence or dishonesty on God's part. It is not really a ruse or trick; it is rather the inability of the prince of this world to understand the divine love. If Satan does not see God, it is because he *is* violent contagion itself. The devil is extremely clever concerning everything having to do with rivalistic conflicts, with scandals and their outcome in persecution, but he is blind to all reality other than that. Satan turns bad contagion into something I hope not to do myself, a totalitarian and infallible theory that makes the theoretician deaf and blind to the love of God for humankind and to the love that human beings share with God, however imperfectly.

Satan himself transforms his own mechanism into a trap, and he falls into it headlong. God does not act treacherously, even toward Satan, but allows himself to be crucified for the salvation of humankind, something beyond Satan's conception. The prince of this world depended too heavily on the extraordinary power of concealment of the victim mechanism.

The Gospels themselves draw our attention to the loss of mythic unanimity everywhere Jesus comes and intervenes. John in particular points out on numerous occasions how the witnesses become divided after Jesus speaks and acts. Each time, the people around Jesus quarrel, and far from unifying them, his message precipitates disharmony and division. In the Crucifixion especially, this division plays a primary role. Without it there would not be a Gospel revelation; the single victim mechanism would not be truthfully represented. It would be, as in the myths, transformed and concealed as just and legitimate action.

Chapter 12

Scapegoat

THE PASSION ACCOUNTS shed a light on mimetic contagion that deprives the victim mechanism of what it needs to be truly unanimous and to generate the systems of myth and ritual: the participants' unawareness of what is driving them. The spread of the message of the Gospels and the entire Bible must therefore bring about first of all the disappearance of archaic religions. And this is what occurs. Wherever Christianity spreads, the mythical systems decay and sacrificial rites disappear. After this disappearance, what does Christianity do in our world? This is just the question that we must now ask.

The complex influence of Christianity spreads in the form of a kind of knowledge unknown to pre-Christian societies, and it continually penetrates them in a more and more profound fashion. This knowledge, which Paul says comes from the Cross, is not esoteric at all. To grasp it, we need only ascertain that we all now observe and understand situations of oppression and persecution that earlier societies did not detect or took to be inevitable.

The biblical and Christian power of understanding phenomena of victimization comes to light in the modern meaning of certain expressions such as "scapegoat." A "scapegoat" is initially the victim in the Israelite ritual that was celebrated during a great ceremony of atonement (Lev. 16:21). This ritual must be very ancient, for it is visibly quite alien to the specifically biblical inspiration as defined in chapters 9 and 10.

The ritual consisted of driving into the wilderness a goat on which all the sins of Israel had been laid. The high priest placed his hands on the head of the goat, and this act was supposed to transfer onto

154

He is interested
why in the
Table of
the Law

the animal everything likely to poison relations between members
of the community. The effectiveness of the ritual was the idea that
the sins were expelled with the goat and then the community was
rid of them.

This ritual of expulsion is similar to that of the *pharmakos* in
Greece, but it is much less sinister because the victim is never a
human being. When an animal is chosen, the injustice seems less, or
even nonexistent. This is no doubt why the scapegoat ritual doesn't
move us to the same repugnance as the "miraculous" stoning instigated by Apollonius of Tyana. But the principle of transference is
no less exactly the same. In a distant period when the ritual was effective as ritual, the transfer of the community's transgressions onto
the goat must have been facilitated by the bad reputation of this
animal, by its nauseating odor and its aggressive sexual drive.

In the primitive and archaic world there are rituals of expulsion
everywhere, and they give us the impression of enormous cynicism
combined with a childish naiveté. In the case of the scapegoat the
process of substitution is so transparent that we understand it at first
glance. It is this comprehension that the modern usage of "scapegoat" expresses; in other words, it is a spontaneous interpretation of
the relationship between the ancient Jewish ritual and transferences
of hostility in our world today. These latter are no longer part of
religious ritual, but they always exist, usually in an attenuated form.

The people participating in rituals did not understand these phenomena as we do, but they observed their reconciling results and
appreciated them so much, as we have seen, that they attempted to
reproduce them without feeling shame. This was the case because
the operation of transferring sins from community to victim seemed
to occur from beyond, without their own real participation.

The modern understanding of "scapegoats" is simply part and
parcel of the continually expanding knowledge of the mimetic contagion that governs events of victimization. The Gospels and the
entire Bible nourished our ancestors for so long that our heritage
enables us to comprehend these phenomena and condemn them.

"But never," you will tell me, "does the New Testament resort to the term 'scapegoat' to designate Jesus as the innocent victim of an escalation of mimetic contagion." You are right, no doubt, but it does use an expression equal and even superior to "scapegoat," and this is *lamb of God.* It eliminates the negative attributes and unsympathetic connotations of the goat. Thereby it better corresponds to the idea of an innocent victim sacrificed unjustly.

Jesus applies another expression to himself that is extremely revealing. It is drawn from Psalm 118: "The stone the builders rejected has become the cornerstone." This verse tells not only of the expulsion of the single victim but of the later reversal that turns the expelled victim into the keystone of the entire community.

In a world where violence is no longer subject to ritual and is the object of strict prohibitions, anger and resentment cannot or dare not, as a rule, satisfy their appetites on whatever object directly arouses them. The kick the employee doesn't dare give his boss, he will give his dog when he returns home in the evening. Or maybe he will mistreat his wife and his children, without fully realizing that he is treating them as "scapegoats." Victims substituted for the real target are the equivalent of sacrificial victims in distant times. In talking about this kind of phenomenon, we spontaneously utilize the expression "scapegoat."

The real source of victim substitutions is the appetite for violence that awakens in people when anger seizes them and when the true object of their anger is untouchable. The range of objects capable of satisfying the appetite for violence enlarges proportionally to the intensity of the anger.

The effectiveness of sacrificial substitutions is increased when many individual scandals come together against one and the same victim. Scapegoat phenomena, therefore, continue to play a definite role in our world at the level of individuals and communities, but they are scarcely studied as such. If we question our sociologists and anthropologists, most of them will recognize the existence and importance of scapegoat phenomena, but they will tell us they aren't sufficiently interested to investigate them. The deeper reason for this attitude is the fear of encountering religion and the sacred, which are really impossible to avoid once we go into the question a little more thoroughly.

Because of Jewish and Christian influence scapegoat phenomena no longer occur in our time except in a shameful, furtive, and clandestine manner. We haven't given up having scapegoats, but our belief in them is 90 percent spoiled. The phenomenon appears so morally base to us, so reprehensible, that when we catch ourselves "letting off steam" against someone innocent, we are ashamed of ourselves.

It is easier than in the past to observe collective transferences upon a scapegoat because they are no longer sanctioned and concealed by religion. And yet it is still difficult because the individuals addicted to them do everything they can to conceal their scapegoating from themselves, and as a general rule they succeed. Today as in the past, to have a scapegoat is to believe one doesn't have any. The phenomenon in question doesn't usually lead any longer to acts of physical violence, but it does lead to a "psychological" violence that is easy to camouflage. Those who are accused of participating in hostile transference never fail to protest their good faith, in all sincerity.

When human groups divide and become fragmented, during a period of malaise and conflicts, they may come to a point where they are reconciled again at the expense of a victim. Observers nowadays realize without difficulty, unless they belong to the persecuting group, that this victim is not really responsible for what he or she is accused of doing. The accusing group, however, views the victim as guilty, by virtue of a contagion similar to what we find in scapegoat rituals. The members of this group accuse their "scapegoat" with great fervor and sincerity. More often than not some incident, whether fantastic or trivial, has triggered a wave of opinion against this victim, a mild version of mimetic snowballing and the victim mechanism.

Metaphorical recourse to this ritual expression, "scapegoating," is often arbitrary in practice, but it rests on a logic that makes sense within its own frame of reference. The similarities are great between phenomena of attenuated expulsion that we observe every day in our world and ancient scapegoat rituals, as well as countless other rituals of the same sort—so great that they must be real. When we suspect people around us of giving in to the temptation of scapegoating, we denounce them indignantly. We ferociously denounce the scapegoating of which our neighbors are guilty, but we are unable to do without our own substitute victims. We all try to tell ourselves that we have only legitimate grudges and justified hatreds, but our feeling of innocence is more fragile than our ancestors'.

We could use our insight discreetly with our neighbors, not humiliating those we catch in the very act of expelling a scapegoat. But more frequently we turn our knowledge into a weapon, a means not only of perpetuating old conflicts but of raising them to a new level of cunning, which the very existence of this knowledge and its propagation in the whole society demand. In short, we integrate the central concern of Judaism and Christianity into our systems of self-defense. Instead of criticizing ourselves, we use our knowledge in bad faith, turning it against others. Indeed, we practice a hunt for scapegoats to the second degree, a hunt for hunters of scapegoats. Our society's obligatory compassion authorizes new forms of cruelty.

St. Paul vividly summarizes this double bind in which we find ourselves in his letter to the Romans: "You have no excuse, O man . . . when you judge another, for in judging you judge yourself, because you, the judge, are doing the very same thing" (2:1). If condemning the sinner is to do the same thing we reprove in him, in both cases the sin in question is nothing else than condemning our neighbor.

The spectacle of secret substitutions, and slipping from one victim to another in a world without ritual permits us to see, in pure form we could say, the functioning of the relational (*interdividual*) mechanisms that underlie the ritual organization of the primitive human world. These mechanisms continue in our world usually as only a trace, but occasionally they can also reappear in forms more virulent than ever and on an enormous scale. An example is Hitler's systematic destruction of European Jews, and we see this also in all the other genocides and near genocides that occurred in the twentieth century. I will say more about this later.

This insight regarding scapegoats and scapegoating is a real superiority of our society over all previous societies, but like all progress in knowledge it also offers occasions to make an evil worse. Let's say I denounce my neighbor's scapegoating with righteous self-satisfaction, but I continue to view my own scapegoats as objectively guilty. My neighbors, of course, don't hold back from denouncing me for the same selective insight that I point out in them.

Scapegoating phenomena cannot survive in many instances except by becoming more subtle, by resorting to more and more complex casuistry in order to elude the self-criticism that follows scapegoaters like their shadow. Otherwise, we could no longer resort to some wretched goat to rid ourselves of our resentments. We now have need of procedures less comically evident.

Jesus makes allusion to this, I think. It is the deprivation of victim mechanisms and its terrible consequences that he talks about when he presents the future of the evangelized world in terms of conflict between persons who are most closely related:

> Don't think that I have come to bring peace on earth; I have not come to bring peace, but a sword. I have come to set a man against his father, and a daughter against her mother, and a daughter-in-law against her mother-in-law. One's enemies will be those of his own household. (Matt. 10:34–36)

In a world deprived of sacrificial safeguards, mimetic rivalries are often physically less violent, but they insinuate themselves into the most intimate relationships. This is what the text I have just quoted specifies: the son at war with his father, the daughter against her mother, etc. The loss of sacrificial protection transforms the most intimate relationships into their exact opposites so that they become relationships of doubles, of enemy twins. This text enables us to identify the true origin of modern "psychology."

THUS THE EXPRESSION "scapegoat" designates (1) the victim of the ritual described in Leviticus, (2) all the victims of similar rituals that exist in archaic societies and that are called rituals of expulsion, and finally (3) all the phenomena of nonritualized collective transference that we observe or believe we observe around us. This last meaning leaps over the barrier that anthropologists attempt to maintain between archaic rituals and their modern substitutes, the phenomena whose persistence shows that, yes, we have changed a little since the time of archaic rituals but less than we would like to believe.

I believe that the modern usage of "scapegoat" is basically valid. This is contrary to anthropologists who want to maintain the illusory autonomy of their discipline and who avoid using the expression "scapegoat" so they won't have to involve themselves in complex analyses that become inevitable when the absolute separation of the archaic and the modern is abolished. My own view is that the modern uses of the term are a sign that the Jewish and Christian revelation is becoming continually more effective and so is far from being a dead letter in our society.

The modern shedding of ritual brings to light the psychosocial substratum of ritual phenomena. We cry "scapegoat" to stigmatize all the phenomena of discrimination—political, ethnic, religious, social, racial, etc.—that we observe about us. We are right. We easily see now that scapegoats multiply wherever human groups seek to lock themselves into a given identity—communal, local, national, ideological, racial, religious, and so on.

The arguments I make are based on the popular insight that crops up in the modern sense of "scapegoat." I am attempting to develop the implications of this insight. It is richer in true knowledge than all the concepts anthropologists, sociologists, and psychologists have invented. All discourses on exclusion, discrimination, racism, etc. will remain superficial as long as they don't address the religious foundations of the problems that besiege our society.

Chapter 13

The Modern Concern for Victims

A BOVE ONE OF THE PORTALS of many medieval churches is a great angel holding a pair of scales. The angel is weighing souls for eternity. If art in our time had not given up expressing the ideas that guide our world, it would rejuvenate this ancient *weighing of souls,* and citizens would have a *weighing of victims* sculpted over the entrance of our parliaments, universities, courts of law, publishing houses, and television stations.

Our society is the most preoccupied with victims of any that ever was. Even if it is insincere, a big show, the phenomenon has no precedent. No historical period, no society we know, has ever spoken of victims as we do. We can detect in the recent past the beginnings of the contemporary attitude, but every day new records are broken. We are all actors as well as witnesses in a great anthropological first.

Examine ancient sources, inquire everywhere, dig up the corners of the planet, and you will not find anything anywhere that even remotely resembles our modern concern for victims. The China of the Mandarins, the Japan of the samurai, the Hindus, the pre-Columbian societies, Athens, republican or imperial Rome—none of these were worried in the least little bit about victims, whom they sacrificed without number to their gods, to the honor of the homeland, to the ambition of conquerors, small or great.

An extraterrestrial who heard our words without knowing any-thing about human history would no doubt imagine that there existed, somewhere in past centuries, a society very superior to ours in terms of compassion. This imagined society must have been so attentive to the sufferings of the unfortunate that it left an undying memory among human beings and that we make it into the fixed star about which our obsession with victims turns. Only our nostalgia for such a society would enable this alien to understand our severity toward ourselves, the bitter reproaches we make to ourselves.

Of course, this ideal society has never existed. Already when Voltaire composed his *Candide* in the eighteenth century, he searched for one and found none superior to the world in which he was living. He therefore had to make up a purely fictional society.

The world in which we live day by day usually doesn't furnish us with satisfying material for condemning ourselves. But that doesn't keep us from repeating, with a hue and a cry against the contemporary world, accusations we know to be false. Never was a society, we often hear, more indifferent to the poor than ours. Yet how could this be, since the idea of social justice, as imperfectly realized as it may be, is found nowhere else? It is a quite recent invention. — *Wrong – see OT Law & prophets*

If I speak as I do, it is not to exonerate our world of all fault. I share the conviction of my contemporaries about its guilt, but I am trying to discover the place and point of view from which we condemn ourselves. I think we have excellent reasons to feel guilty, but they are certainly not the ones we state.

To justify the curses we rain upon ourselves, it is not enough to realize that we are the richest and best equipped of all the societies in history. The rich and powerful were not lacking even in the most miserable societies, and they showed utter indifference to the countless victims about them. Our world must be under an injunction that it imposes on itself. The generations just preceding us already heard the same summons, but it wasn't nearly as loud and urgent. The more we go back in time, the weaker the summons sounds. This suggests that in the future it will become even louder. Since we cannot pretend to hear nothing, we condemn our deficiencies, but we don't know why or in the name of what. We pretend to believe that what summons us is something everyone has always heard, but in reality we are the only ones who hear it.

By comparison to the means at our disposal our good deeds are insignificant, it is true; our failures are horrible. We have good reasons to blame ourselves, but where do they come from? The worlds that preceded us shared our concern, our worry, and our solicitude so little that they weren't sensitive enough to reproach their own indifference. If we question our historians, they will invoke modern humanism and other ideas of the same kind that enable them never to mention religion and to say nothing about the role of Christianity. The latter, supposedly null and void, can hardly have failed to play a role in the origin of these ideas.

In France humanism developed in opposition, of course, to the Christianity of the prerevolutionary regime, which was accused of complicity with those in power, and quite rightly so. From one country to the other the sudden turns of fortune are different, but they cannot conceal the true origin of our modern concern for victims; it is quite obviously Christian. Humanism and humanitarianism develop first on Christian soil.

Nietzsche proclaimed vigorously against the hypocrisy of his own time, which was basically the same as our own but not as gross. Nietzsche, the most anti-Christian philosopher of the nineteenth century, identified the source of our guilt in an era when it was less evident than today. It was already a caricature of Christianity but less caricaturally obvious than today.

If there is a Christian ethic as such, it is essentially love of one's neighbor or charity in the old Christian sense. It is not hard to locate its origin:

> "Come, O blessed of my Father, inherit the kingdom prepared for you since the foundation of the world: for I was hungry and you gave me to eat, I was thirsty and you gave me to drink, I was a stranger and you welcomed me, naked and you clothed me, sick and you visited me, in prison and you came to see me." Then the righteous will answer him, "Lord, when did we see you hungry and feed you, thirsty and give you to drink, a stranger and welcome you, naked and clothe you, sick or in prison and visit you?" And the King will answer them, "Truly, I say to you, as you did it to one of the least of these my brothers, you did it to me." (Matt. 25:34–40)

Jb?
Jeremiah?
Amos?

The idea of a society alien to violence goes back clearly to the preaching of Jesus, to his announcement of the kingdom of God. This ideal does not diminish to the extent that Christianity recedes; to the contrary, its intensity increases. The concern for victims has became a paradoxical competition of mimetic rivalries, of opponents continually trying to outbid one another.

The victims most interesting to us are always those who allow us to condemn our neighbors. And our neighbors do the same. They always think first about victims for whom they hold us responsible.

We do not all have the same experience as St. Peter and St. Paul, who discovered that they themselves were guilty of persecution and confessed their own guilt rather than that of their neighbors. It's our neighbors who kindly remind us that we should be compassionate, and we render them the same service. In our world, in short, where we are all bombarding each other with victims, the final result is what Christ announced in words that the modern concern for victims clarifies for the first time:

> "The blood of all the prophets, shed since the foundation of
> the world, may be required of this generation, from the blood
> of Abel to the blood of Zechariah." (Luke 11:50–51)

This teaching has come to be verified with a considerable delay from the schedule the first Christians anticipated, but the important thing is not the date of the verification, but that it is verified.

From now on we have our antisacrificial rituals of victimization, and they unfold in an order as unchangeable as properly religious rituals. First of all we lament the victims we admit to making or allowing to be made. Then we lament the hypocrisy of our lamentation, and finally we lament Christianity, the indispensable scapegoat, for there is no ritual without a victim, and in our day Christianity is always it, *the scapegoat of last resort.* As part of this last stage of the ritual, we affirm, in a nobly suffering tone, that Christianity has done nothing to "resolve the problem of violence."

In our perpetual comparisons between our world and the others of the past, we always use two weights and two measures. We do everything possible to conceal the overwhelming superiority of our world, which, in any case, is in competition only with itself as it takes in the entire planet. Whether we examine the matter attentively or not, we easily see that everything people say about our world is true: it is by far the worst of all worlds. They say repeatedly—and this is not false—that no world has made more victims than it has. But the opposite proposition is equally true: our world is also and by far the best of all worlds, the one that saves more victims than any other. In order to describe our world, we must multiply all sorts of propositions that should be incompatible but now are true simultaneously.

The concern for victims leads us to the sound opinion that our progress in "humanitarianism" is very slow and we should certainly not glorify it, in order not to slow it down even more. The modern concern for victims obligates us to blame ourselves perpetually. Our concern for victims is characteristically never satisfied with past successes. It never praises itself or tolerates its own praise. It tries to turn attention away from itself because we should be attentive only to victims. Our concern denounces its own laxity, its Pharisaism. Our concern for victims is the secular mask of Christian love.

In short, what prevents us from examining our concern for victims too closely is this concern itself. Whether this humility is feigned or sincere, it is compulsory in our world, and there is no doubt that it stems from Christianity. The concern for victims does not operate on the basis of statistics. It operates on the Gospel principle of the lost sheep for whom the shepherd will abandon all his flock if need be.

To prove to ourselves that we are really neither ethnocentric nor triumphalist, we thunder against the bourgeois self-satisfaction of the last century, we ridicule the foolishness of so-called progress, and we fall into the opposite foolishness: we confess to being the most inhumane of all societies. Yet modern democracies can defend themselves by pointing to a mass of accomplishments so unique in human history that they are the envy of the rest of the world.

The gradual loosening of various centers of cultural isolation began in the Middle Ages and has now led into what we call "globalization," which in my view is only secondarily an economic phenomenon. The true engine of progress is the slow decomposition of the closed worlds rooted in victim mechanisms. This is the force that destroyed archaic societies and henceforth dismantles the ones replacing them, the nations we call "modern."

SINCE THE FASHION is one of weighing victims, let's play the game without cheating. Let's examine first the scale that holds our successes: since the High Middle Ages all the great human institutions have evolved in the same direction: more humane private and public law, penal legislation, judicial practice, the rights of individuals. Everything changed very slowly at first, but the pace has been accelerating more and more. When viewed in terms of the large picture, this social and cultural evolution goes always in the same direction, toward the mitigation of punishment, greater protection for potential victims.

Our society abolished slavery as well as serfdom. Later has come the protection of children, women, the aged, foreigners from abroad, and foreigners within. There is also the battle against poverty and "underdevelopment." More recently we have made medical care and the protection of the handicapped universal.

Every day we cross new thresholds. When a catastrophe occurs at some spot on the globe, the nations that are well off feel obligated to send aid or to participate in rescue operations. You may say these gestures are more symbolic than real and reflect a concern for prestige. No doubt, but in what era before ours and under what skies has international mutual aid constituted a source of prestige for nations?

There is just one rubric that gathers together everything I am summarizing in no particular order and without concern for completeness: the concern for victims. This concern sometimes is so exaggerated and in a fashion so subject to caricature that it arouses laughter, but we should guard against seeing it as only one thing, as nothing but twaddle that's always ineffective. It is more than a hypocritical comedy. Through the ages it has created a society incomparable to all the others. It is unifying the world for the first time in history.

How have all these things actually come to pass? In each generation legislators questioned more radically an ancestral heritage that they felt was their duty to transform. Where their ancestors saw nothing to be reformed, they discovered oppression and injustice. The status quo had long appeared untouchable, determined by nature or intended by the gods, even by the Christian God. For centuries successive waves of concern for victims have revealed and restored new types of scapegoats at the lowest levels of society. Only a few spiritual geniuses in the past suspected that the unjust sufferings of these scapegoats could be eliminated.

The modern concern for victims comes to the forefront for the first time, I think, in the religious institutions we call "charitable." This begins, it seems, with the "house of God,"[1] that extended arm of the Church that quickly became the *hospital.* The hospital welcomes all the crippled and ill without distinction of social, political, or even religious identity. Inventing the hospital meant dissociating for the very first time the idea of victim from all concrete ethnic, regional, or class identity. It is the invention of the modern victim concept.

The cultures that were still autonomous cultivated all sorts of solidarity—familial, tribal, and national—but they did not recognize the victim as such, the anonymous and unknown victim, in the sense in which we say "the unknown soldier." Prior to this discovery there was no humanity in the full sense except within a fixed territory. Today all these local, regional, and national identities are disappearing: "Ecce homo."[2]

The essential thing in what goes now as human rights is an indirect acknowledgment of the fact that every individual or every

---

1. The term in French is *l'Hotel-Dieu,* which has no exact equivalent in English. It is the name of the most ancient hospital in Paris. The author's point is that the creation of such a house where the sick and wounded are cared for is the first of its kind in history. It evolved into the modern hospital. — Trans.

2. "Behold the man!" This is the Roman governor Pontius Pilate's exclamation about Jesus as he appears before a crowd that shouts for his crucifixion. — Trans.

group of individuals can become the "scapegoat" of their own community. Placing emphasis on human rights amounts to a formerly unthinkable effort to control uncontrollable processes of mimetic snowballing.

What we have a foreboding of, at least vaguely, is the possibility that any community whatever may persecute its own members. This happens whenever crowds mobilize suddenly against anyone, anywhere, anytime, in any way, no matter what the pretext. It also happens, more frequently, when societies become permanently organized on a basis that privileges the few at the expense of the many, when unjust forms of social life continue for centuries, even for millennia. The concern for victims seeks to protect us against the countless varieties of the victim mechanism.

The most effective power of transformation is not revolutionary violence but the modern concern for victims. What pervades this concern and makes it effective is a true knowledge of oppression and persecution. It seems that this knowledge was at first very limited, and then it became bolder by virtue of its early successes. To summarize this knowledge, we must return to the analyses of the preceding chapter: it is the knowledge that separates the ritual meaning of the expression "scapegoat" from its modern meaning. It deepens continually, and soon the mimetic reading of the structure of persecution will become more and more widespread.

The evolution I am rather haphazardly summarizing forms the basis of the effort of our societies to eliminate the permanent scapegoat structures that form their foundation, and this occurs to the extent that we become aware of their existence. This transformation comes across as a timeless moral imperative. Societies that did not see the need for transforming themselves are nonetheless altered, always in the same direction, in response to the desire to make amends for past injustices and to bring about more "humane" relations among their members. Each time a new frontier is crossed, those whose interests are damaged oppose this change intensely. But once the situation has been altered, the results are never seriously contested.

In the eighteenth and nineteenth centuries some people realized that this evolution was on the way to creating a group of nations whose uniqueness in terms of progress was further enhanced by their rapidly accelerating technological and economic progress. It was mostly the privileged classes, of course, that benefited from this technological and economic progress, and they fell into an overweening pride and extraordinary insolence. It is possible to view the great catastrophes of the twentieth century as in part the inevitable punishment of this pride and insolence.

We can compare ancient societies to one another, but the global society now in the making is truly unique. Its superiority in every area is so overwhelming, so evident, that it is forbidden, paradoxically, to acknowledge the fact, especially in Europe. This prohibition stems from the fear of a return to tyrannical pride. It is also the fear of humiliating nations that don't belong to the privileged group. In other words, it is once again the concern for victims that dominates what it is permissible and impermissible to say.

Our society perpetually confesses to crimes and faults of which it is certainly guilty when considered against our absolute standard, but it is innocent relative to all the other types of societies. We certainly have not ceased being "ethnocentric." But it is evident also that we are the least ethnocentric of all societies in history. We are the ones who invented the concept five or six centuries ago—Montaigne's chapter on the "cannibals" is proof of that. To be capable of such an invention, it is necessary no doubt to be less ethnocentric than other societies, which are so exclusively preoccupied with themselves that they never forged the notion of ethnocentrism. Even if our self-criticism is superficial, we are the only society that ever invented this unique intellectual activity.

Our world did not invent compassion, it is true, but it has universalized it. In archaic cultures it was practiced within extremely circumscribed groups. Their borders were always marked by victims. Mammals mark their territorial borders with their excrement. Human beings have long done the same thing with that particular form of excrement that we call their scapegoats.

Chapter 14

The Twofold Nietzschean Heritage

I N OUR WEIGHING OF SOULS, let us now scrutinize the balance scales of our defects, our faults, our failures. If we gain great advantages from our liberation from scapegoats and sacrificial rituals, this freedom is also the occasion of oppression and countless persecutions. It is a source of peril and the danger of destruction.

For centuries the justice we owe to the concern for victims has freed our energies, increased our potentials. But this concern presents temptation to which we usually succumb, such as colonial conquests, abuses of power, the murderous wars of the twentieth century, the pillage of the planet, etc.

As I see it, of all the disasters of the last two centuries the most horrible is the systematic destruction of the Jewish people by German National Socialism. Of course massacres are common in human history, but they are generally conceived in the heat of action and are immediate acts of vengeance, a ferocious spontaneity. When they are premeditated, we usually have little trouble identifying their objectives.

Hitler's genocide of the Jews is another matter. Certainly it's part of a long history of anti-Semitic persecutions in Christian Europe, but this evil tradition does not explain everything. Something escapes the usual criteria in this project of annihilation, so meticulously conceived and executed. It didn't serve the German war objectives but worked to their disservice.

Hitler's genocide flagrantly contradicts the thesis argued in the preceding chapter that the Western world, and now effectively the entire planet, is dominated by the concern for victims. This contradiction should compel me to change my views or to make it the basis of my entire interpretation of the genocide. The second solution is the good one, I believe. The spiritual goal of Hitler's ideology was to root out of Germany, then all of Europe, that calling that the Christian tradition places upon all of us: the concern for victims.

For evident tactical reasons, Nazism at war attempted to conceal the genocide. I think that if it had won out, it would have announced it publicly in order to show that Nazism had ended the concern for victims as the supposedly irrevocable sense of our history.

But to suppose, as I do, that the Nazis clearly found in the concern for victims the dominant value of our world, isn't this to overestimate their moral and spiritual insight? I believe not. They found support in the thinker who discovered the anthropological key to Christianity: its vocation of concern for victims. I refer, of course, to Friedrich Nietzsche.

Nietzsche was the first philosopher to understand that the collective violence of myths and rituals (everything he named "Dionysos") is of the same type as the violence of the Passion. The difference between them is not in the *facts*, which are the same in both cases, but in their interpretation.

The anthropologists investigating primitive societies were too positivist, too confident in the evidence of facts by themselves, to comprehend the distinction between facts and their interpretation, how they are *represented*. In our days the "deconstructionists"[1] reverse the positivist error. For them, only interpretation exists. They want to be more Nietzschean than Nietzsche. Instead of getting rid of problems of interpretation, they get rid of facts.

In certain unedited writings just before his final breakdown, Nietzsche escapes the twin errors of the positivists and the nihilists,

---

1. "Deconstruction" is a method of criticizing or taking apart texts, ideas, and convictions that are based on traditional forms of thinking that have a "foundation" or some sort of sacred center. It is particularly associated with Jacques Derrida, who holds that any traditional notion of representing some original thing, event, or other reality is no longer possible. Girard admires his analysis of the Greek *pharmakon*, which means both "poison" and "remedy." However, he is opposed to the deconstructionist approach of continually cutting up and undercutting all texts (and anything that lays claim to a "foundation") and asserting that there is no reference in a text except to itself and other texts. — Trans.

and he discovers the truth that I only repeat after him, the truth that dominates this book: in the Dionysian *passion* and in the *Passion* of Jesus there is the same collective violence. But the interpretation is different:

> Dionysos versus the "Crucified": there you have the antithe-
> sis. It is not a difference in regard to their martyrdom—it is
> a difference in the meaning of it. Life itself, its eternal fruit-
> fulness and recurrence, creates torment, destruction, the will
> to annihilation. In the other case, suffering—the "Crucified as
> the innocent one"—counts as an objection to this life, as a
> formula to its condemnation.[2]

Between Dionysos and Jesus there "is not a difference in regard to their martyrdom." In other words, the accounts of the Passion recount the same kind of drama as the myths, but the "meaning" is different. While Dionysos approves and organizes the lynching of the single victim, Jesus and the Gospels disapprove.

This is exactly what I have said and keep on saying: myths are based on a unanimous persecution. Judaism and Christianity destroy this unanimity in order to defend the victims unjustly condemned and to condemn the executioners unjustly legitimated.

As incredible as it may seem, no one made this simple but funda-mental discovery before Nietzsche—no one, not even a Christian! So on this particular point we must give Nietzsche his just due. But beyond this point, sad to say, the philosopher becomes deliri-ous. Rather than recognizing the reversal of the mythic scheme as an indisputable truth that only Judaism and Christianity proclaim, Nietzsche does all he can to discredit the Christian awareness that this type of victim is innocent.

He sees perfectly well that one is dealing with the same vio-lence in both cases ("there is not a difference in regard to their martyrdom"), but he doesn't see or want to see the injustice of the violence. He doesn't see or want to admit that the unanimity al-

---

2. Friedrich Nietzsche, *The Will to Power*, ed. Walter Kaufmann (New York: Vintage Books, 1967), 542–43.

ways prevailing in the myths has to be based on mimetic contagion, which possesses the participants and which they don't recognize, whereas the Gospels recognize and denounce violent contagion, as do the story of Joseph and the other great biblical texts.

Nietzsche, to discredit the Jewish-Christian revelation, tries to show that its commitment to the side of victims stems from a paltry, miserable resentment. Observing that the earliest Christians belonged primarily to the lower classes, he accuses them of sympathizing with victims so as to satisfy their resentment of the pagan aristocrats. This is the famous "slave morality."

So this is how Nietzsche understands the "genealogy" of Christianity! He opposes, so he believes, the crowd mentality, but he does not recognize his Dionysian stance as the supreme expression of the mob in its most brutal and its most stupid tendencies.

Christianity does not yield to ulterior motives of resentment in its concern to rehabilitate victims. It is not seduced by a contaminated charity of resentment. What it does is to rectify the illusion of myths; it exposes the lie of the "satanic accusation."

Since Nietzsche is blind to mimetic rivalry and its contagion, he doesn't see that the Gospel stance toward victims does not come from prejudice in favor of the weak against the strong but is heroic resistance to violent contagion. Indeed, the Gospels embody the discernment of a small minority that dares to oppose the monstrous mimetic contagion of a Dionysian lynching.

Nietzsche had to trick himself to avoid clearly seeing this. To escape the consequences of his own discovery and persist in a desperate negation of the biblical truth of the victim, Nietzsche resorts to an evasion so gross, so unworthy of his best thinking, that his mind could not hold out against it. For it is not by accident, in my view, that the explicit discovery of what Dionysos and the Crucified have in common and what separates them occurs so shortly before his final breakdown. Nietzsche's devotees try to empty his insanity of all meaning. We can understand perfectly why. The nonsense of madness plays a protective role in their thought just as madness itself functions for Nietzsche. Nietzsche the philosopher was unable to sit back comfortably in the monstrosities into which the need to minimize his discovery was driving him. And so he took refuge in madness.

Christian truth has been making an unrelenting historical advance in our world. Paradoxically, it goes hand in hand with the apparent decline of Christianity. The more Christianity besieges our world, in the sense that it besieged Nietzsche before his collapse, the more difficult it becomes to escape it by means of innocuous painkillers and tranquilizers such as the "humanistic" compromises of our dear old positivist predecessors.

To elude his own discovery and to defend mythological violence, Nietzsche is obliged to justify *human sacrifice,* and he doesn't hesitate to do so, resorting to horrifying arguments. He raises the stakes even on the worst social Darwinism. He suggests that to avoid degenerating, societies must get rid of humans who are waste, who hinder and weigh them down:

> Through Christianity, the individual was made so important, so absolute, that he could no longer *be sacrificed:* but the species endures only through human sacrifice. . . . Genuine charity demands sacrifice for the good of the species—it is hard, it is full of self-overcoming, because it *needs human sacrifice.* And this pseudo-humaneness called Christianity wants it established that *no one should be sacrificed.*[3]

Weak and ill as he was, Nietzsche never misses an occasion to flagellate our modern concern for the weak and the ill. A true Don Quixote of death, he condemned every measure in favor of the disinherited. In attacking the concern for victims, he denounced the cause of what he took to be the precocious aging of our civilization, the acceleration of our decadence. But this thesis doesn't even deserve to be refuted. Not only has the Western world not aged rapidly, but it seems to have extraordinary longevity, due to renewal and perpetual enhancement of its leadership and institutions.

---

3. Ibid., 142, emphasis mine.

The Gospel defense of victims is certainly more humane than Nietzsche's thought, but we should not see in this a distortion of some "hard truth." It is Christianity that holds on to the truth against Nietzschean madness.

By insanely condemning the real greatness of our world, not only did Nietzsche destroy himself, but he suggested the terrible destruction that was later done by National Socialism. The Nazis perceived acutely that the grotesque "genealogy" of Nietzsche would not be enough to vanquish the Judeo-Christian tradition. The Nazis could not wait for the superior human, Nietzsche's Overman, to emerge through peaceful historical events. After their conquest of power, they disposed of resources much superior to those of an unhappy philosopher gone mad.

To bury the modern concern for victims under millions and millions of corpses—there you have the National Socialist way of being Nietzschean. But some will say, "This interpretation would have horrified poor Nietzsche." Probably, yes. Nietzsche shared with many intellectuals of his time and our own a passion for irresponsible rhetoric in the attempt to get one up on opponents. But philosophers, for their misfortune, are not the only people in the world. Genuinely mad and frantic people are all around them and do them the worst turn of all: they take them at their word.

Since the Second World War a whole new intellectual wave has emerged, hostile to Nazism but more nihilist than ever, more than ever a tributary of Nietzsche. It has accumulated mountains of clever but false arguments to acquit its favorite thinker of any responsibility in the National Socialist catastrophe. But still, Nietzsche is the author of the only texts capable of clarifying the Nazi horror. If there is a spiritual essence of the movement, Nietzsche is the one who expresses it.

Intellectuals of the postwar period cheerfully conjured away the texts I have just quoted. They felt they were in some way authorized by the real successor of Nietzsche, the semiofficial interpreter of his thought in the eyes of the everlasting avant-garde: Martin Heidegger. Since before the war this profound thinker had

cast a prudent prohibition over the Nietzschean version of philosophical neo-paganism. He excommunicated Nietzsche's reflection
on Dionysos and the Crucified, minimizing it, dismissing it (not
without cunning) as a simple mimetic rivalry between Nietzsche
and "Jewish monotheism."

Heidegger prohibited the study of these texts without ever dis-
avowing their content. To identify and condemn the inhumanity
of what was happening around him was not his strong point, as
everyone knows. But his authority has not suffered. During the second half of the twentieth century it remained so great that even
until recently no one dared transgress Heidegger's censorship of the
religious problematic that Nietzsche articulated.

IN SPITE OF ITS VICTIMS without number, Hitler's murderous enterprise ended in failure. It has had a twofold effect: it has accelerated
the concern for victims, but it has also demoralized it. Hitlerism
avenges its failure by making the concern for victims hysterical,
turning it into a kind of caricature. Yet in a world where relativism
has seemingly defeated religion and every "value" that is religious
in origin, the concern for victims is more alive than ever.

The proud optimists of the eighteenth and nineteenth centuries
thought they alone were responsible for scientific and technological
progress, but a dark pessimism took over the second half of the twentieth century. Although understandable, this reaction is as excessive
as the arrogance preceding it.

We live in a world, as I have pointed out, that constantly
reproaches its own violence, and it does this systematically and ritu-
alistically. We are always prepared to translate all our conflicts, even
those that don't lend themselves at all to it, into the language of innocent victims. The debate over abortion, for example: whether we
are for it or against it, we always have to choose our side in the interest of the "real victims." Who deserves our sympathy more—the
mothers who sacrifice themselves for their children or the children
sacrificed to contemporary pleasure-seeking and "self-fulfillment"?
There you have the question.

The nihilisms of the extreme left are just as partial to Nietzsche as the nihilisms of the extreme right, but they carefully refrain from reviving the real Nietzschean enterprise, which was to demolish our modern concern for victims. Since the failure of Nazism no deconstructionist or demystifier has attacked that value. And yet in Nietzsche's eyes the destiny of his thought was at stake in that deconstruction, in that demystification.

SINCE THE CONCERN for victims becomes widespread only in the modern world, we might think that it would marginalize us in relation to the past, but this is not so. It is the concern for victims that marginalizes the past. We hear repeated in every way that we no longer have an absolute. But the inability of Nietzsche and Hitler to demolish the concern for victims and then later the embarrassed silence of the latter day Nietzscheans show for sure that this concern is not relative. It is our absolute.

No one has achieved success in making the concern for victims "outdated," and this is because it's the only thing in our world that is not the creation of current fashion (although fashions often arise from it). The rise of "victim power" coincides, not at all by accident, with the arrival of the first planetary culture. To designate a permanent, unchangeable dimension of human existence, the existentialist philosophers spoke of *care* or *concern*.[4] This is the usage I have in mind as I take up this term. I connect it with *modern* to underline the paradox of a value whose recent historical arrival in no way prevents it from asserting itself as the immutable and eternal.

There were those who told us not long ago that human life existed in an absolute void of meaning. True enough, the old absolutes have collapsed—humanism, rationalism, revolution, science itself. And

---

4. I have translated *le souci* in this chapter usually as "concern" in the phrase "the concern for victims" (*le souci des victimes*). The word became well known primarily in Heidegger's work, where *die Sorge* is a central theme of his analysis of what constitutes *Dasein*, which is distinctively human existence. *Die Sorge* is usually translated "care," though in German it may mean "anxiety," "grief," "worry." Likewise, the French *souci* usually has a stronger sense than the English "concern," with the connotation of "solicitude" or sometimes "anxiety." Girard's phrase *le souci des victimes* could be rendered "the care of victims" or "caring (solicitude) for victims," but "concern for victims" is more idiomatic. It is the phrase he always uses when he writes in English. — Trans.

yet even today this absolute void does not prevail. There is the concern for victims, and it is that value, for better or for worse, that dominates the total planetary culture in which we live.

The world becoming one culture is the fruit of this concern and not the reverse. In all the areas of activity—economic, scientific, artistic, and even religious—it is the concern for victims that determines what is most important. This new stage of culture has come about due neither to scientific progress nor to the market economy nor to the "history of metaphysics."

What was enduring in the now defunct ideologies was this concern, still clothed in philosophical irrelevancies. In our day everything has opened up, and the concern for victims appears in broad daylight, in all its purity and impurity. We can see, but only with the advantage of hindsight, that for centuries it has directed the evolution of our world behind the scenes. If the concern for victims has fully appeared, it is because all the great expressions of modern thought are exhausted and discredited. After all the ideological collapses, our intellectuals believed they could settle down into the easy life of a nihilism without obligations or sanctions. But our nihilism is a pseudo-nihilism. To believe in it as real, we have to try to take the concern for victims as self-evident, a feeling so universal and innate that it should not be identified as a value. To the contrary, it is really an obvious exception to our emptiness of value. The wilderness certainly surrounds it, but this is true in all the worlds in which an absolute is dominant.

WHAT ONLY THE GREAT INSIGHT of a Nietzsche could formerly perceive, now even a child can perceive. The current process of spiritual demagoguery and rhetorical overkill has transformed the concern for victims into a totalitarian command and a permanent inquisition. The media themselves notice this and make fun of "victimology," which doesn't keep them from exploiting it. The fact that our world has become solidly anti-Christian, at least among its elites, does not prevent the concern for victims from flourishing—just the opposite.

The majestic inauguration of the "post-Christian era" is a joke.

We are living through a caricatural "ultra-Christianity" that tries to escape from the Judeo-Christian orbit by "radicalizing" the concern for victims in an anti-Christian manner.

Belief systems based on illusory transcendence are in process of disintegrating throughout the world under the impact of the Christian revelation. This disintegration entails the retreat of religion almost everywhere, and this includes, paradoxically, the retreat of Christianity itself because "sacrificial" vestiges from the past have contaminated it for such a long time that it remains vulnerable to the attacks of numerous enemies.

The influence of Nietzsche is very much present in our world. Many intellectuals, when they turn to the Bible or the New Testament, claim to smell there (with a disgust borrowed of course from Nietzsche) what they call "des relents du bouc émissaire" ("the odor of the scapegoat").[5] They find this smell "nauseating," and I suppose this is in memory of the original he-goat. These fine bloodhounds never exercise this exquisite acuteness of their sense of smell when they turn to Dionysos and Oedipus. No one ever detects in the myths the stench of corpses badly buried. The myths are never the objects of the least suspicion.

Since the Renaissance, paganism has enjoyed among our intellectuals a reputation for transparency, sanity, and health that nothing can shake. Paganism is favorably perceived as always opposed to everything "unhealthy" that Judaism and Christianity impose.

Up to and including Nazism, Judaism was the preferential victim of this scapegoat system. Christianity came only in second place. Since the Holocaust, however, it is no longer possible to blame Jews. The intellectuals and other cultural elites have promoted Christianity to the role of number one scapegoat. Everyone goes into ecstasy over the airy, wholesome, athletic character of Greek civilization, as against the supposedly closed, suspicious, dull, and repressive atmosphere of the Jewish and Christian world. This is the ABCs of the universities as well as the link between the Nietzscheism of National

---

5. The French has no exact equivalent in English. *Le relent* refers to a bad odor that persists, usually associated with mold, must, or staleness. — Trans.

Socialism and the Nietzscheism of Heidegger and his followers. Both share this deep hostility to our religious traditions.

If our world were really to escape the influence of Christianity, it would have to renounce the concern for victims. Nietzsche and Nazism understood this well. They hoped to relativize Christianity, expose it as a religion like all the others, just a little worse. As such it could be replaced either by atheism or by a quite new religion, completely foreign to the biblical legacy. Heidegger had not abandoned all hope of a complete extinction of Christian influence and a new start at zero, which would begin a new mimetic cycle. This is the sense, I think, of the most celebrated line in Heidegger's "last testament" interview, published in *Der Spiegel* after his death: "Only a god can save us."

The attempt by Nietzsche and Hitler to make humankind forget the concern for victims has ended in a failure that seems definitive, at least for the moment. But it is not Christianity that profits from the victory of the concern for victims in our world. It is rather what I think must be called *the other totalitarianism,* the most cunning and malicious of the two, the one with the greatest future, by all evidence. At present it does not oppose Judeo-Christian aspirations but claims them as its own and questions the concern for victims on the part of Christians (not without a certain semblance of reason at the level of concrete action, given the deficiencies of historical Christianity). The other totalitarianism does not openly oppose Christianity but outflanks it on its left wing.

All through the twentieth century, the most powerful mimetic force was never Nazism and related ideologies, all those that openly opposed the concern for victims and that readily acknowledged its Judeo-Christian origin. The most powerful anti-Christian movement is the one that takes over and "radicalizes" the concern for victims in order to paganize it. The powers and principalities want to be "revolutionary" now, and they reproach Christianity for not defending victims with enough ardor. In Christian history they see nothing but persecutions, acts of oppression, inquisitions.

This other totalitarianism presents itself as the liberator of humanity. In trying to usurp the place of Christ, the powers imitate him in the way a mimetic rival imitates his model in order to defeat him. They denounce the Christian concern for victims as hypocritical and a pale imitation of the authentic crusade against oppression and persecution for which they would carry the banner themselves.

In the symbolic language of the New Testament, we would say that in our world Satan, trying to make a new start and gain new triumphs, borrows the language of victims. Satan imitates Christ better and better and pretends to surpass him. This imitation by the usurper has long been present in the Christianized world, but it has increased enormously in our time. The New Testament evokes this process in the language of the *Antichrist*. To understand this title, we should de-dramatize it, for it expresses something banal and prosaic.

The Antichrist boasts of bringing to human beings the peace and tolerance that Christianity promised but has failed to deliver. Actually, what the radicalization of contemporary victimology produces is a return to all sorts of pagan practices: abortion, euthanasia, sexual undifferentiation, Roman circus games galore but without real victims, etc.

Neo-paganism would like to turn the Ten Commandments and all of Judeo-Christian morality into some alleged intolerable violence, and indeed its primary objective is their complete abolition. Faithful observance of the moral law is perceived as complicity with the forces of persecution that are essentially religious. Since the Christian denominations have become only tardily aware of their failings in charity, their connivance with established political orders in the past and present world that are always "sacrificial," they are particularly vulnerable to the ongoing blackmail of contemporary neo-paganism.

Neo-paganism locates happiness in the unlimited satisfaction of desires, which means the suppression of all prohibitions. This idea acquires a semblance of credibility in the limited domain of consumer goods, whose prodigious multiplication, thanks to technological progress, weakens certain mimetic rivalries. The weakening of mimetic rivalries confers an appearance of plausibility, but only that, on the stance that turns the moral law into an instrument of repression and persecution.

Conclusion

anthropology

AS ALREADY NOTED, Simone Weil suggests that the Gospels are
a theory of humankind even before they are a theory of God.
Even though she sees no role for the Hebrew Bible, the positive
aspect of her insight corresponds to what we have discovered in
this series of analyses.

To understand this evangelical anthropology, we must complete
it with the Gospel statements concerning Satan. Far from being absurd or fantastic, they use another language to reformulate a theory
of scandals and the working of a mimetic violence that initially decomposes communities and subsequently recomposes them, thanks
to the unanimous scapegoating triggered by the decomposition.

In all the titles and functions attributed to Satan, we see re-
appearing all the symptoms of desire and its sickness, the evolution
of which Jesus diagnoses. These titles and functions include the
"tempter," the "accuser," the "prince of this world," the "prince of
darkness," the "murderer from the beginning," and all of them together explain why Satan is the concealed producer-director of the
Passion.

This dynamic concept of Satan enables the Gospels to articulate
the founding paradox of archaic societies. They exist only by virtue
of the sickness that should prevent their existence. In its acute crises
the sickness of desire generates its own antidote, the violent and
pacifying unanimity of the scapegoat. The pacifying effects of this
violence continue in the ritual systems that stabilize human communities. All of this is epitomized in the statement "Satan expels
Satan."

The Gospel theory of Satan uncovers a secret that neither ancient nor modern anthropologies have ever discovered. Violence in archaic religion is a temporary remedy. The sickness is not really cured and always recurs in the end.

To identify Satan as mimetic violence completes the process of discrediting the prince of this world; it puts the finishing touch on Gospel demystification; it contributes to that "fall of Satan" that Jesus announces before his crucifixion. The revelatory power of the Cross dispels the darkness that the prince of this world must have to preserve his power to make us believe he really exists.

With regard to anthropology, the Gospels are like a road map of mimetic crises and their mythical-ritual resolution. They are a guide that enables us to travel about in archaic religion without losing our way.

THERE ARE ONLY TWO WAYS of relating the sequence of a mimetic crisis and its violent resolution: the true and the false.

1. We don't detect the mimetic snowballing because we participate in it without realizing it. In this case we are condemned to a lie we can never rectify, for we believe sincerely in the guilt of our scapegoats. This is what myths do.

2. We detect the mimetic snowballing in which we do not participate, and then we can describe it as it actually is. We restore the scapegoats unjustly condemned. Only the Bible and the Gospels are capable of this.

We must perceive this common occurrence of mimetic crises and the scapegoating they produce, behind myths and the Bible, in order to perceive as well the unfathomable abyss that separates mythology from Judaism and Christianity. This abyss is the insurmountable difference between falsehood and the truth to which Judaism and Christianity lay claim. We defined this difference first by comparing and contrasting Joseph to Oedipus, then a second time by comparing and contrasting the Gospels to all mythology.

The Judeo-Christian difference is one the first Christians felt almost physically. In our day it is hardly still felt, but look how we become capable of defining it when we compare the relevant texts! We then make the evidence for this difference clear at the level of anthropological analysis and define it in a rational way.

THE WORD OF THE GOSPEL is unique in really problematizing human violence. All other sources on humankind resolve the question of violence before it is even asked. Either the violence is considered divine (myths), or it is attributed to human nature (biology), or it is restricted to certain people or types of persons only (who then make excellent scapegoats), and these are ideologies. Or yet again violence is held to be too accidental and exceptional for human knowledge to consider. This last position is our good old philosophy of Enlightenment.

As we stand before Joseph, on the other hand, or before Job, before Jesus, before John the Baptist and still other victims, we wonder why so many mobs expel and massacre so many innocent persons. Why are so many communities caught up in madness?

The Christian revelation clarifies not only everything that comes before it, the religion and culture of myth and ritual, but also everything that comes after, the history we are in the process of making, the ever-growing disintegration of archaic religion, the opening into a future joining all humankind into one world. It is more and more liberated from ancient forms of servitude, but by the same token, it is deprived of all sacrificial protection.

The knowledge we have acquired about our violence, thanks to our religious tradition, does not put an end to scapegoating but weakens it enough to reduce its effectiveness more and more. This is the true reason why *apocalyptic* destruction threatens us, and this threat is not irrational at all. The rationality enters more profoundly every day into the concrete facts of contemporary history, questions of armament, ecology, population, etc.

The theme of apocalypse has an important role in the New Testament. It is not at all the mechanical repetition of Jewish preoccupations that would make no sense in our world. This is what

Albert Schweitzer thought, and many biblical scholars continue to assert it. To the contrary, apocalyptic is an integral part of the Christian message. If we are not aware of this, then we amputate something essential from this message and destroy its coherence. The preceding analyses lead to a purely anthropological and rational interpretation of apocalyptic expectations, an interpretation that does not ridicule them but understands their relevance.

By revealing the secret of the prince of this world, the Passion accounts subvert the primordial source of human order. The darkness of Satan is no longer thick enough to conceal the innocence of victims who become, at the same time, less and less "cathartic." It is no longer possible really to "purge" or "purify" communities of their violence. Satan can no longer expel Satan. We should not conclude from this that humans are going to be immediately rid of their now fallen prince.

In the Gospel of Luke Christ sees Satan "fall like lightning from heaven" (10:18). Evidently he falls to earth, and he will not remain inactive. Jesus does not announce the immediate end of Satan, not yet at least. It is rather the end of his false transcendence, his power to restore order through his false accusations, the end of scapegoating.

The New Testament has quite a repertory of metaphors to signify the consequence of the Christian revelation. We can say about Satan, as I've stated, that he can no longer expel himself. We can say likewise that he can no longer "bind himself," which amounts basically to the same thing. As the days of Satan are numbered, he tries to gain the most from them, and quite literally, he unleashes himself.

Christianity expands the range of freedom, which individuals and communities make use of as they please, sometimes in a good way but often in a bad way. A bad use of freedom contradicts, of course, what Jesus intends for humanity. But if God did not respect the freedom of human beings, if he imposed his will on them by force or even by his prestige, which would mean by mimetic contagion, then he would not be different from Satan.

Jesus is not the one who rejects the kingdom of God; it's human beings who do so, including a number of those who believe they are nonviolent simply because they benefit to the utmost from the protection of the principalities and powers, and so they never have to use force themselves. Jesus distinguishes two types of peace. The first is the peace that he offers to humanity. No matter how simple its rules, it "surpasses human understanding" because the only peace human beings know is the truce based on scapegoats. This is "the peace such as the world gives." It is the peace that the Gospel revelation takes away from us more and more. Christ cannot bring us a peace truly divine without depriving us first of the only peace at our disposal. His peace entails this troubling historical process through which we are living.

What delays the "unbinding of Satan"? St. Paul, in the letter to the Thessalonians, defines it as a *katechon,* as that which *contains* the Apocalypse in the twofold sense of the word as noted by J. P. Dupuy: to have within itself and to hold within certain limits. This "containing" is made up of a set of qualities that contradict one another, and in particular the force stemming from the inertia of the powers of this world, their inability to understand the Revelation of Christ in spite of their worldly intelligence and adaptability.[1]

True demystification has nothing to do with automobiles and electricity, contrary to what Bultmann imagined. Real demystification comes from our religious tradition. We "moderns" believe we possess intuitive knowledge solely because we are completely immersed in our "modernity." Let us not confuse true enlightenment with the idolatry of the here and now.

Why is the true principle of demystification stated fully only in one religious tradition, the Christian tradition? Isn't this intolerably unfair in the era of "pluralisms" and "multiculturalisms"? Isn't the main thing to make no one jealous or envious? Aren't we supposed to sacrifice truth to the peace of the world in order to avoid

---

1. On this subject, see the essay by Wolfgang Palaver, "Hobbes and the *Katechon*: The Secularization of Sacrificial Christianity," in *Contagion* (spring 1993): 57–74.

the terrible wars of religion for which we must get ready everywhere, so it is said, if we are going to defend what we believe to be
the truth?

To respond to these questions I will let Giuseppe Fornari speak:

> The fact that we possess a cognitive tool unknown to the
> Greeks does not mean we have the right to think ourselves bet-
> ter than they and the same is true in regard to non-Christian
> cultures. Christianity's power of penetration has not been its
> particular cultural identity but its capacity to redeem the whole
> history of man, summing up and surpassing all its sacrificial
> forms. This is the real spiritual metalanguage that can describe
> and go beyond the language of violence. . . . This explains the
> prodigiously rapid spread of Christianity in the pagan world,
> absorbing the living force of its symbols and customs.[2]

TRUTH IS EXTREMELY RARE on this earth. There even arise occasions to think that it may be completely absent. Events of mimetic
escalation are indeed, by definition, unanimous. Each time one occurs it overwhelms all the witnesses without exception. It makes
unshakable false witnesses of all the members of the community, for
they become incapable of perceiving the truth. Given the power of
violent contagion, the secret of Satan should be safe from any revelation. There are only two possibilities when scapegoating threatens.
Either the victim mechanism will be triggered, and its unanimity eliminates all lucid witnesses. Or it will not be triggered, and
the witnesses will remain lucid but will have nothing to reveal.
Under normal conditions the victim mechanism is unknowable,
undiscoverable. The secret of Satan is inviolable.

Contrary to all other phenomena, whose fundamental attribute is
that of appearing (the word "phenomenon" comes from the Greek
phainesthai: shine, appear), the victim mechanism of necessity disappears behind the mythic meanings it produces. It is therefore

---

2. Giuseppe Fornari, "Labyrinthine Strategies of Sacrifice: *The Cretans* by Euripides,"
Contagion (spring 1997): 187.

paradoxical, exceptional, unique as a phenomenon. The inviola-
bility of this mechanism explains the extreme assurance of Satan
prior to the Christian revelation. The master of the world believed
he would be forever able to hide his secret from prying glances and
to preserve intact the instrument of his domination. And yet he was
wrong. In the end, as we've seen, he was "duped by the Cross."

In order for the Gospel revelation to occur, it's necessary that
the violent contagion against Jesus be both unanimous and not
unanimous. It must be unanimous for the mechanism to work, and
yet the unanimity must fail in the end for the mechanism to be
unveiled. These two conditions are not realizable simultaneously,
but they can be fulfilled one after the other. This is evidently what
happened in the case of the Crucifixion, what finally made it possible
for the victim mechanism to be revealed.

When Jesus is arrested, Judas has already betrayed him; the disciples flee; Peter is about to deny his master. The mimetic contagion
appears at the point of toppling, as usual, into unanimity. If that
had occurred, if the violent contagion had triumphed, there would
be no Gospel. There would only be one more myth.

But on the third day of the Passion the scattered disciples re-
group again about Jesus, who they believe is risen from the dead.
Something happens in extremis that never happens in myths. A
protesting minority appears and resolutely rises up against the unanimity of the persecuting crowd. The latter becomes no more than
a majority, numerically overwhelming, of course, but incapable from
now on of totally imposing its conception of what has happened, its
mythical *representation* of the Crucifixion.

The protesting minority is so minuscule, so lacking in prestige,
and above all so late in forming that it doesn't affect at all the
working of the single victim mechanism. However, its heroism will
enable it not only to continue but to write, or be responsible for the
writing of, the accounts that will be told and proclaimed throughout
the world and that will spread everywhere the subversive knowledge
of scapegoats unjustly condemned.

During the Passion, the little group of Jesus' last faithful followers was already more than half-possessed by the violent contagion against Jesus. Where did they suddenly find the strength to oppose the crowd and the Jerusalem authorities? How do we explain this turnabout so contrary to all we have learned of the irresistible power of mimetic escalation?

Until now I have always been able to find plausible responses to the questions posed in this book within a purely commonsensical and "anthropological" context. This time, however, *it is impossible.* To break the power of mimetic unanimity, we must postulate a power superior to violent contagion. If we have learned one thing in this study, it is that none exists on the earth. It is precisely because violent contagion was all-powerful in human societies, prior to the day of the Resurrection, that archaic religion divinized it. Archaic societies are not as stupid as we tend to think. They had good reasons to mistake violent unanimity for divine power.

The Resurrection is not only a miracle, a prodigious transgression of natural laws. It is the spectacular sign of the entrance into the world of a power superior to violent contagion. By contrast to the latter it is a power not at all hallucinatory or deceptive. Far from deceiving the disciples, it enables them to recognize what they had not recognized before and to reproach themselves for their pathetic flight in the preceding days. They acknowledge the guilt of their participation in the violent contagion that murdered their master.

WHAT IS THIS POWER that triumphs over mimetic violence? The Gospels respond that it is the Spirit of God, the third person of the Trinity, the Holy Spirit. The Spirit takes charge of everything. It would be false, for example, to say the disciples "regained possession of themselves": it is the Spirit of God that possesses them and does not let them go.

In the Gospel of John the name given to this Spirit admirably describes the power that tears the disciples away from this all-powerful contagion: the Paraclete. I have commented on this term in other essays, but its importance for what I am doing in this book is so great that I must return to it. The principal meaning of *parakletos* is "lawyer for the defense," "defender of the accused." In place of looking for periphrases and loopholes to avoid this translation, we should prefer it to all others and marvel at its relevance. We should take with utmost seriousness the idea that the Spirit enlightens the persecutors concerning their acts of persecution. The Spirit discloses to individuals the literal truth of what Jesus said during his crucifixion: "They don't know what they are doing." We should also think of the God whom Job calls "my defender."

The birth of Christianity is a victory of the Paraclete over his opposite, Satan, whose name originally means "accuser before a tribunal," that is, the one responsible for proving the guilt of the defendants. That is one of the reasons why the Gospels hold Satan responsible for all mythology. The Passion accounts are attributed to the spiritual power that defends victims unjustly accused. This corresponds marvelously to the human content of the revelation, to the extent that violent contagion permits it to be understood.

The anthropological revelation is not prejudicial to the theological revelation or in competition with it. It is inseparable from it. This union of the two is demanded by the dogma of the Incarnation, the mystery of the double nature of Jesus Christ, divine and human. The "mimetic" reading permits a better realization of this union. The anthropological widening of the Incarnation in no way eclipses theology; it shows its relevance by putting the abstract idea of original sin into more concrete form, as James Alison has powerfully observed.[3]

To HIGHLIGHT THE ROLE of the Holy Spirit in the defense of victims, it will be useful, finally, to take a look at the parallelism of two great conversions that occur in conjunction with the Resurrection. The first is Peter's repentance after his denial, so important that we can view it as a second and more profound conversion. The other is the conversion of Paul, his famous "road to Damascus" experience.

On the surface these two events seem completely different: they don't occur in the same texts, and one happens at the very begin-

---

3. James Alison, *The Joy of Being Wrong* (New York: Crossroad, 1998).
O.P. (formerly)   *See p. 21 n.*

ning, the other at the end of the crucial period of Christianity's infancy. Their circumstances are very different. The two men are very different. But the profound meaning of the two experiences is nonetheless exactly the same. What the two converts become capable of seeing, thanks to their conversions, is the violent social instinct, the adherence to the will of the crowd, which neither knew possessed him. This is the violent contagion that compels us all to participate in the Crucifixion.

Just after his third denial Peter hears a rooster crow, and he remembers what Jesus predicted. Only then does he discover the crowd phenomenon in which he has participated. He proudly believed he was immunized against all unfaithfulness to Jesus. All through the Gospel accounts Peter is the ignorant instrument of scandals that manipulate him without his knowledge. In speaking to the Jerusalem crowd some days after the Resurrection, he stresses the *ignorance* of those possessed by violent contagion. He speaks from personal knowledge.

In the Gospel of Luke, just at the crucial moment, Jesus too is in the courtyard, and the two—Jesus and Peter—exchange a look that pierces the disciple's heart. The question that Peter reads in this look, "Why do you persecute me?" Paul will hear as well from Jesus' own mouth: "Saul, Saul, why do you persecute me?" In response to Paul's question "Who are you, Lord?" Jesus answers, "I am Jesus whom you persecute." Christian conversion is always this question that Christ himself asks. Because of the simple fact that we live in a world whose structure is based on mimetic processes and victim mechanisms, from which we all profit without knowing it, we are all accessories to the Crucifixion, persecutors of Christ.

The Resurrection empowers Peter and Paul, as well as all believers after them, to understand that all imprisonment in sacred violence is violence done to Christ. Humankind is never the victim of God; God is always the victim of humankind.

My research is only indirectly theological, moving as it does across the field of a Gospel anthropology unfortunately neglected by theologians. To increase its effectiveness, I have pursued it as long as possible without postulating the reality of the Christian God. No appeal to the supernatural should break the thread of the anthropological analyses.

By offering a natural, rational interpretation of facts formerly perceived as relevant to the supernatural, such as Satan or the apocalyptic dimension of the New Testament, the mimetic reading truly enlarges the field of anthropology. But contrary to non-Christian anthropologies it does not minimize the hold evil has on humans and their need for redemption. Certain Christian readers fear that this enlargement encroaches on the legitimate domain of theology. I believe the opposite is true. By desacralizing certain themes, by showing that Satan exists first of all as a figure created by structures of mimetic violence, we think with the Gospels and not against them.

This enlargement of anthropology occurs, we must observe, at the expense of subjects that current theologians, even the most orthodox, have a tendency to neglect, as they can no longer integrate them into their work. They do not want to reproduce, purely and simply, ancient readings that don't desacralize violence sufficiently. Neither do they want to suppress the basic texts under an imperative of "demythologizing" that is positivist and naïve, in the manner of Bultmann. So they remain silent. The mimetic interpretation opens a way out of this impasse.

Far from minimizing Christian transcendence, attributing purely earthly, rational meanings to themes such as Satan or apocalyptic danger renders Paul's "paradoxes" of the Cross more relevant than ever. I think that through our engagement with some of the most astonishing texts of Paul we have already found enlightenment for the true demythicizing of our world, and we will find enlightenment even more in the future, as Gil Bailie foresees.[4] This enlightenment can only come from the Cross.

---

4. Gil Bailie, *Violence Unveiled* (New York: Crossroad, 1995).

For the word of the cross is folly to those who are perishing, but for those who are being saved, for us, it is the power of God. For it is written, *"I will destroy the wisdom of the wise, and the cleverness of the clever I will thwart."* Where is the sage? Where is the scribe? Where is the debater of this age? Has not God made foolish the wisdom of the world? For since the world, in the wisdom of God, did not recognize God by means of wisdom, it has pleased God to save those who believe by the folly of preaching. For the Jews demand signs and the Greeks seek wisdom, but we preach Christ crucified, a scandal to the Jews and folly for the Gentiles, but for those who are called, Jews as well as Greeks, it is Christ who is the power of God and the wisdom of God. For the foolishness of God is wiser than men, and the weakness of God is stronger than men.

(1 Cor. 1:18–25, emphasis mine)

Index

disciples, the: betrayal by, xix, 19; the Holy Spirit and, 189–90; as a key element in subverting the victim mechanism, x, xix, xxi, 2, 124, 149, 188–89; mimetic contagion and, 24; scandal and, 23–24
divinity, 131–36. *See also* gods, pagan
doubles, 22, 22n.2, *159*
double transference/transformation, xvi, 67, 72
Dreyfus case, 145–46
Dupuy, J. P., 186
Durkheim, Emile, 100

Egypt, 82
elderly, the, 166   *Enlightenment, The 184*
Eliade, Mircea, 83, 86
Ephesus, stoning at. *See* Apollonius of Tyana
ethnocentrism, 169
Eucharist, xiv
Eusebius of Caesarea, 54
euthanasia, 181
Exodus, the, xx
exorcism, 38

Fall, the, 7
false transcendence, 96, 96n.1, 97, 98, *185*
first stone, the, 55–56
Fornari, Giuseppe, 187
founding murder, the: the basis of cultural institutions and, 91–94; comparative study of, 82–83; myths of, xv–xvi; the Old Testament and the theme of, 83–85; religion's persistent importance and, 87–91; the Roman Empire and, 98–99
Freud, Sigmund, 144
functionalism, 93   *freedom 185*

genocide, 159, 170
Germanic peoples, 82
Gernet, Louis, 65
globalization, 166, 169, 178
God: the duping of Satan and, 151–52; Jesus and the imitation of, 13–14; uniqueness of Israel's view of, xvii–xviii. *See also* gods, pagan; Holy Spirit, the; Jesus Christ
gods, pagan: current misunderstanding of the true nature of, 74; the miracle of Apollonius of Tyana and, 66–69; myths turning victims into, 65–66; postmodernism's misunderstanding of, 119–20; process by which human victims become, xvi–xvii, 123; and reasons for sacrifice, 79–80
Goodhart, Sandor, 78
Gospels, the: anthropology and, 21, 103–4, 183; anti-Semitism and, 25–26; comparison of the Old Testament and myth with, 121–22; desire in, 7; on false and

true manifestations of the divine, 131–36; founding murder in, 85–87; mythology contrasted with, xiv, 1, 2, 104–6; the Old Testament and, 127–30; the persecutory unconscious and, 126–27; the psalms and, 127–28; representation of the single victim mechanism in, 143–48; on scandal, 16–17; uniqueness of the message of, xviii–xix, 2–3, 122–25
Greece, 51–52, 76–78, 81. *See also* Apollonius of Tyana
Greek Fathers, 149

handicapped persons, 166
Heidegger, Martin, xxiin.2, 175–76, 177n.4, 180
Heracles, 67, 68
Heraclitus, 120
Herod, 27, 132, 133–34, 135–36
Herodias, 27
heroes, x
Hitler, Adolf, 158–59, 170, 176
Hobbes, Thomas, 8
Holocaust, the, 159, 170–71
Holy Spirit, the, 2–3, 189–90
hospitals, 167, 167n.1
humanism, 163
humanitarianism, 163
human rights, 167–68   *ideology 184*
idolatry, 118–19, 151, *96–7, 186*
imitation, 13–15, 40
Imitation of Christ (Thomas à Kempis), 13
Incarnation, the, 43–44, *190*   *? imago Dei*
India, 82
individualism, 20 *11, 14, 42, 96*
instinct, x, xv, 11, 15, 90, 93, 94, 215
institutions, 88–91
interdividual, the, 137n.2   *irony 143*
Islam, 122

Jacob, xvii, 111, 112
Jesus Christ: Apollonius of Tyana compared with, 54–58, 59–61; and concern for the victim as the new absolute value, xx–xxi, xxiii; contrast of his death with that of other scapegoats, 2–3; imitation and, 13–15; and the Law on stoning, 58–59; and the modern world's view of victims, 163–64; the Old Testament and, 127–30; on peace, 186; scandal and, 16–17, 23; the "triumph of the Cross" and, 139–43; uniqueness of, xix, 122–25
Job, xviii, 117–18
John the Baptist, 27–28, 133–36

revelation
18
186, 190

[handwritten: / assoc w/ darkness 183, 185]

[handwritten: suspicion 145]

Of Related Interest

Revelation, the Religions, and Violence
by Leo D. Lefebure
ISBN 1-57075-300-8, paperback

Revelation, the Religions, and Violence examines the basic
human dynamics that produce violence and how the diverse
experiences of Christianity, Judaism, and Islam, as well as
Chinese and Indian religions, address this universal problem.
Leo Lefebure extends the path-breaking insights of
René Girard into a multireligious context.

Please support your local bookstore, or call 1-800-258-5838

For a free catalog, please write us at
Orbis Books, Box 308
Maryknoll, NY 10545-0308
or visit our website at www.orbisbooks.com

Thank you for reading *I See Satan Fall Like Lightning.*
We hope you enjoyed it.